Money and Banking

DANTES/DSST* Study Guide

All rights reserved. This Study Guide, Book and Flashcards are protected under the US Copyright Law. No part of this book or study guide or flashcards may be reproduced, distributed or stored in a retrieval system, or transmitted in any form or by any means, electronic, mechanical, photocopying, recording, or otherwise, without the prior written permission of the publisher Breely, Crush & Associates LLC.

© 2011 Breely, Crush & Associates, LLC

*DSST is a registered trademark of The Thomson Corporation and its affiliated companies, and does not endorse this book.

Copyright ©2003 - 2011, Breely Crush Publishing.

All rights reserved.

This Study Guide, Book and Flashcards are protected under the US Copyright Law. No part of this publication may be reproduced, distributed or stored in a retrieval system, or transmitted in any form or by any means, electronic, mechanical, photocopying, recording, or oherwise, without the prior written permission of the publisher Breely Crush Publishing.

Published by Breely Crush Publishing
10808 River Front Parkway
South Jordan, UT 84095
www.breelycrushpublishing.com

ISBN-10: 1-61433-057-3
ISBN-13: 978-1-61433-057-8

Printed and bound in the United States of America.

*DSST is a registered trademark of The Thomson Corporation and its affiliated companies, and does not endorse this book.

Table of Contents

1.0 The Origin and Evolution of Money 1
    1.1 Barter 1
    1.2 Money as an IOU 2
    1.3 The Basic Properties of Money 2
    1.4 Bills of Exchange 2
    1.5 Paper Money 3
    1.6 Goldsmith Bankers 3
    1.7 Virginian Tobacco 3
    1.8 Gold Standard 4
    1.9 Intangible Money 5
    1.10 The Future of Money 5

2.0 A Brief History of Banking and Credit 7
    2.1 The Fractional Reserve System 9
    2.2 What is a bank? 10
    2.3 How banks create money 10

3.0 The Contemporary World Financial System 12
    3.1 Components of the contemporary financial system 13
    3.2 The International Monetary Fund (IMF) 13
    3.3 Bank of International Settlements (BIS) 14
    3.4 The World Bank 15
    3.5 Central Banks -The U.S. Federal Reserve Bank System 16
    3.6 Investment Banks and Commercial Banks 18
    3.7 Government Sponsored Entities (GSEs) 18
    3.8 Stock, Foreign Exchange (FOREX) and Commodity Exchanges 19
    3.9 Some concerns 22

4.0 The Role of Interest Rates 23
    4.1 Effects of Inflation 23
    4.2 Time Value of Money 24
    4.3 The Influence of Interest Rates 27
    4.4 The U.S. Federal Reserve Bank and how interest rates are determined .. 29
    4.5 The Federal Funds rate and Reserve Requirement 29
    4.6 Other important types of financial interest rates 31

5.0 Banking and Indirect Finance 33
    5.1 How a bank functions 33
    5.2 Types of Banks 35

- 5.3 How do Banks Make Money? 36
- 5.4 Corporate Formation and Structure of Banks 38
- 5.5 Obtaining a mortgage and an auto loan 41
- 5.6 Bank Operations 43

6.0 Non-Bank Finance 45
- 6.1 Public market financing 45
- 6.2 Private Investment Companies and Syndicates 45
- 6.3 Venture capitalists 45
- 6.4 Leasing companies 45
- 6.5 Private or second mortgages 46
- 6.6 Sub-Prime mortgage lending 46
- 6.7 Asset-Based Lending 47

7.0 Central Banking 47
- 7.1 Brief History of the U.S. Federal Reserve Bank 48
- 7.2 Structure of the Federal Reserve System 49
- 7.3 Role of the FOMC and how Fed Funds rates are established 50
- 7.4 How the Fed Funds rate affects retail loan rates 52
- 7.5 How the Fed funds rate affects Aggregate Demand for Goods and Services 53
- 7.6 Constant Vigilance 54
- 7.7 The U.S. dollar and the lender of last resort (LOLR) 55
- 7.8 Fed Controversy 56

8.0 International Finance 57
- 8.1 International Trade, Comparative Advantage and Exchange rates 57
- 8.2 Currency Exchange Rates 58
- 8.3 Foreign Investment 62
- 8.4 Balance of Payments 64
- 8.5 Balance of Payments Deficit and Surplus 65
- 8.6 The International Financial System 66
- 8.7 Monetary Policy and Globalization 66
- 8.7 Conclusion 67

Appendix A 68
Sample Test Questions 70
Test-Taking Strategies 95
Test Preparation 95
Legal Note 96

 1.0 The Origin and Evolution of Money

Most archeologists believe that money got its start from cultural customs. Quotes from the Old Testament of the Bible command "an eye for an eye" for a measure of basic justice. You take an eye, you give an eye. Importantly, the old law was a proscription for payment for "blood money events." Once adopted by the ancients, it became a custom perhaps even stronger than law.

The ancients also established payments for certain other events such as:

- Dowries for the payment for the lost services of daughters who were married off. In this case, local custom usually provided for the gifting of items of value and use such as cattle, sheep, grain, gold, etc. to the soon to be deprived families of the bride
- Taxes and Tribute were imposed by conquerors and kings to exact payment (spoils to the victors) or provide for the common good. These payments varied in form depending on what was considered to have value and countable quantity (Pillaging, rape and plunder were tactics of war- not a payment)
- Gifts to the Gods were usually made of something of great value
- Gift giving as a custom required giving something of value

Customary payments were usually not codified but known through local custom.

1.1 BARTER

In ancient times, Barter was the main method for exchanging one thing of value for another thing of value. Of course, the problem with barter is determining value. Each individual barter transaction is a special situation and lacks standardization. Trading cattle, sheep and other animals had tremendous variation: How does one value a scrawny horse compared with a sleek one? Every transaction had variation and a need for the added value of "negotiating expertise," which could make a big difference in the outcome. But, in the end, the transaction usually filled the requirement of satisfying both buyer and seller. As more and more transactions took place between cultures, there became a need to develop a better way to standardize value across cultures. Moreover, barter transactions made trade cumbersome in that most things of value were not easily transportable (usually animals like cattle, horses and sheep) and could also become objects inciting raids and creating political tensions.

As trade increased more and more cultures began to place a common value on certain objects that could function as a store of value. Items such as tools, shells, weapons, spices, and beads helped trade to move from barter to a more standardized method of payment.

Unfortunately, mankind being what it is, counterfeiters soon began to undermine the methods of payment. Swords were made with inferior metals; spices were diluted with inferior herbs, and so on. In 640-630 B.C., the Lydians began minting uniform pieces of silver as a means of exchange and value became a matter of authenticity and weight of minted coins. Subsequently, traders throughout Asia Minor began using coinage. As coinage expanded, so did trade.

1.2 MONEY AS AN IOU

If traders agree to receive equivalent value *at a later date* in exchange for other goods, they establish a form of *credit* to be paid later; the traders have accepted an IOU as a means of facilitating a transaction. The IOU becomes a credit for the seller – to be paid to the seller at a later date – and it becomes a debt to the buyer to be paid to the seller at a later date. If the IOU is accepted as a payment by the seller to a third party, the IOU is considered as *negotiable*. The ability for a negotiable IOU to be accepted by others is a requirement for something to be considered as money.

1.3 THE BASIC PROPERTIES OF MONEY

Money is an object that acts as a unit of value. An IOU will be accepted in exchange for goods and services only if it is seen as a store of value. In sum, *money is usually portable and a store of value*. Moreover, money enables us to measure the value of a good or service against another, based on what each sells for on the market. For example, how many units of money are equivalent in value to a haircut can only be determined in the marketplace.

1.4 BILLS OF EXCHANGE

With the onset of the Crusades in the 10th century, written instructions in the form of *bills of exchange* came to be used as a means of transferring large sums of money. The *Knights Templar* and *Hospitallers* (both were armed religious sects) evolved into bankers to help sustain the years of crusade activities far away from the sources of funding. Both groups acted on behalf of the church and nobles back in Europe to pay for wages and supplies in the Holy Land. As a result of their banking activities, the Knights Templar (said to be the founders of the Free Masons) became one of the strongest financial institutions of the time until the 13th century, when the King of France, who owed a fortune in borrowed funds to the Templars, put most of them to death with the full backing of the Catholic Church. Exactly where the vast sums of Templar funds ended up is still a matter of legend and fodder for modern-day conspiracy theories.

1.5 PAPER MONEY

Paper money was introduced in China around the beginning of the 10th century AD. It was written that the Emperor Hien Tsung mandated the use of paper money when a replacement was needed to supplement the dwindling supply of copper used in coins. A short time after the inception of paper money, the Emperor overprinted the paper money in an effort to pay-off potential invaders with the fiat money and the result was the first recorded evidence of inflation caused by government abuse of the printing press. Subsequent Chinese history reveals several periods of hyper-inflation and in 1455 China abandoned paper money. Today, paper money is the main medium of exchange for daily individual transactions; however, digital entries of credits and debts are by far the main medium of exchange for larger transactions. As new portable technology becomes practical and acceptable, digital money may replace paper and coinage altogether. In fact, some citizens feel that the threat of terrorism and money launderers may be helping to expedite the transition to total digital money as governments and taxation authorities quietly push for the acceptance of digital money as a means for tighter control.

1.6 GOLDSMITH BANKERS

Around the mid 17th century, European jewelers and goldsmiths began acting as agents for storing wealth and the issue of credit. Goldsmiths and jewelers routinely used safes and employed secure procedures to safeguard their stores of gold and jewels. A common practice evolved – particularly in England – whereby clients would safeguard deposits of gold and jewels by renting space in the safes of their local jeweler's or goldsmith's storage facilities. Soon, clients began instructing their jewelers or goldsmiths to pay money to other customers using written instructions backed by the security of what was on deposit with the merchants. These instructions became standardized as this form of transaction grew popular and goldsmiths created standardized instructions for payment to third parties. This process developed into what was called a *banknote*. These banknotes were a form of *monetizing* deposits made by the client and not only served as deposit receipts but also provided clients the ability to pay debts to third parties.

1.7 VIRGINIAN TOBACCO

In the 18th century, during England's period of colonizing the Americas, a severe shortage of official coinage led to various substitutes for money. In Virginia, tobacco leaves were used as *fiat money* but each leaf had to have a certificate attesting to the quantity and quality of the tobacco leaves deposited in warehouses. These certificates were used as paper money backed by a commodity with specific value.

1.8 GOLD STANDARD

As various forms of money were used in a multitude of circumstances, it became clear that if there were no controls on quantity and quality, money could be created like alchemists aspire to turn lead into gold. However, following the model used by the goldsmith-bankers of having a quantifiable and tangible commodity backing the value of money, gold and silver began to be used in tandem with the issuance of paper representations of value. The *convertibility* of a banknote (the ability to exchange a banknote into a specific amount of gold or silver) gave the notes value and the step of exchanging the note for the gold could be bypassed and save a step in the transaction process. All holders of gold-backed notes knew that the note could be exchanged at anytime and assured the value of the paper note. This is called a *gold-backed currency*.

However, during the Napoleonic Wars, the Bank of England suspended the convertibility of its banknotes. This lifted all backing restraints and, as has happened many times with other episodes of unbacked paper money issued in time of war, inflation started to increase (the value of paper money decreased in value and would purchase less) and concerns were expressed about the lack of control over the amount of the money put into circulation. In 1816, recommendations were made by a special committee that Britain readopt the gold standard for their currency (the pound). The pound was originally an amount of silver weighing – you guessed it – a pound. France and the United States also were in favor of a bimetallic standard (either silver or gold) and in 1867 an international conference was held in Paris to try to extend the area of common currencies based on coins with standard weights of gold and silver. However, when the various German states merged into a single country in 1871 they chose the gold standard. The Scandinavian countries adopted the gold standard shortly afterwards. France made the switch from bimetallism to gold in 1878 and Japan, which had been on a silver standard, changed in 1897. Finally, in 00, the United States officially adopted the gold standard. However, within a short span of 20-30 years, Britain, France, and many other countries who had earlier switched to a gold-backed currency broke with gold convertibility once again.

After the Second World War, because the American economy was about the only economy left intact, the US dollar replaced the British pound sterling as the global currency. As the US currency was still backed by gold, other countries pegged their exchange rates to the US dollar. In other words, countries without transparency or regulations were able to keep the same stability of the U.S. dollar without the constraints. However, in 1973 during the Nixon administration, the United States broke with the gold standard as the world's system of fixed exchange rates began to break down.

1.9 INTANGIBLE MONEY

As Thomas Petzinger said: "Today most of the money in the world isn't even made of paper, much less metal. It exists as binary digits. No wonder the central banks of the world are heaving their gold reserves into a collapsing market. Who needs gold when money sheds the slightest pretense of being anything but data? Say good-bye to gold. Gold is history. If you want currency backed by something tangible, sign up for 5,000 frequent flier miles on a new Visa card."

Once money broke with any sort of convertibility, perceived value has carried the day. Value of any currency is now determined by a global and loosely defined network of currency traders who digest all the numerous macro-micro economic factors that can affect a nation's currency. Each second of every working day, trillions of dollars worth of currency contracts are priced, bought and sold. It's not exactly a free market, but much closer to it than the market has been in the past. Traders rate the value of a nation's currency by deciding at what price to buy or sell a particular currency and then a comparative domino effect spills over to all other currencies. For example, on the FOREX (Foreign Exchange Market), the major currency pairs are bought and sold in a complex system of bid and ask pricing. Prices instantly flash across computer screens around the world. An important industry – totally independent from central banks – has come into being to judge the worthiness of a nation's currency. Trade balances, monetary and fiscal policies, economic indicators, weather, crop reports, political events and thousands of other variables are analyzed by individual speculators, banks, commodity traders and central banks; the cumulative verdict is revealed in spot and future currency prices. The value of most major currencies is now a matter of consensus.

1.10 THE FUTURE OF MONEY

Paul Hartzog, in *The Future of Money*, creates a possible scenario for the future. "You go to a rock concert, and you've never seen the opening band before. You like their music, so you get on your mobile device (PDA, cell phone, etc.) and hit the band's 'mobile commerce' exchange. Your software negotiates with their software to determine what currencies they accept and what currencies your various bank accounts carry, including automatically getting you the best currency exchange rate at that instant. The system discovers that because they are opening for a major musician who has his own currency based on his popularity, the opening band has agreed to accept the headliner's currency for the duration of the show for people who are actually at the concert. You verify that you are there using some kind of brokered authentication (GPS or a ticket number); the two systems complete the transaction for you, and you have access to the music."

New forms of money are rapidly making their appearance on the economic landscape. Frequent Flyer Miles – a form of money issued by private corporations – is one of the largest "local currencies" in existence spawned by clever marketing executives and issued to loyal customers. The Information Age has spawned other new kinds of currencies such as "Netmarket Cash" for Internet commerce. Even Alan Greenspan, past Chairman of the Federal Reserve, foresees "new private currency markets in the 21st century."

The LETSystem – Local Exchange Trading System – is said to be the most advanced form of local currency in circulation today. The basic concept behind LETS is that conventional money, while easy to spend, is hard to earn. As a result, LETS advocates believe that money is coercive by nature – people with money exercise power over people without it.

LETS uses a revolutionary social view of money, which puts moral value on the local currency. Specifically, the LETS model stipulates that there's an ample supply of money and nobody really *needs it*, so things only happen when people want them to happen. People either serve willingly, or not at all. Nobody can tell anyone else what to do. If everybody has enough money to live on, money loses its coercive power. According to LETS, if a person has lots of local currency it only represents wealth earned by what others want to give to others in the local community. Acknowledgement in local money has value because that money represents the commitment of people in the community, to the community. LETS could be described as a form of social welfare where each individual can decide what real interests they have and either make more money or earn no additional money but live a lifestyle they prefer. In other words, LETS tries to take the desperation out of the pursuit of money.

A currency used in a specific geographic locale is considered to be a *local currency*. Today, however, technology – namely the Internet – frees up the constraint on a geographical location. For example, a buyer in India can instantaneously purchase an item valued in a "local currency" via the Internet using a credit card or PayPal, which will make the instantaneous exchange of Indian Rupees to whatever local currency is needed to make the purchase.

The only potential restrictions to the definition of what constitutes a currency of exchange will be the world's governments. Most constitutions and government regulations mandate the particular government – local in nature – establish, print and regulate its local currency. However, the free movement of digital credits and debits may eventually become a catalyst for a "one world currency" as trade across borders grows in volume and importance. Moreover, the creation of digital money may make it much easier for governments to monitor transactions of any kind and greatly improve the ability to collect taxes and control money laundering. As the saying goes, "whoever controls the money holds the power" and there is little doubt that using a sophisticated and complicated system of money based upon bytes and not paper would appeal to most taxing and law enforcement authorities around the world.

Bernard Lietaer, author of *The Future of Money and Credit,* suggests that complimentary currencies don't have to be necessarily small scale social affairs. If implemented correctly, they could potentially play a role in a much larger economic arena as well. So it's possible there could be an explosion of currencies instead of the consolidation of a "world currency." The challenge will be maintaining an open currency system as opposed to one that is monopolized by private corporations or governments. As the old saying goes, "he who controls the money, controls the power."

Needless to say, the evolution of money is likely to continue and pick up speed as the world becomes more connected by the Internet. As a matter of fact, with money laundering and terrorist financing in the spotlight, some believe that official paper money might be phased out in favor of completely digital credits that must pass through a federal or world clearing agency. It's fairly obvious that there appears to be a set of events moving toward a head-on collision: a consolidation of world currencies, or an expansion of local currencies and multiple ways of placing value for the exchange of goods or services.

 2.0 A Brief History of Banking and Credit

In the historical context, banking actually preceded coinage. The concept of banking got its start in ancient Mesopotamia where temples and palaces had a role in the storage of grain. During ancient times, payments for taxes and general storage were commonly made in grain. Usually the only structures large enough to store the harvest were in the largest structures in the community- the temples and palaces. Over 3,000 years ago, individual farmers who stored their grain, received a receipt in the form of a clay tablet written in cuneiform with a royal seal. As custom helped to establish the reliability of the clay receipts, eventually they became transferable as payments to third parties. For example, if farmer Abraham promised a portion of his grain harvest as part of the dowry for his new third wife, he could make a contract in favor of the father of the bride and the management of the storage facility could issue a credit receipt secured by farmer Abraham's grain storage in the facility. Thus, temples and palaces became the first banks. Eventually, private houses started to rent out space for grain storage and banking became widespread. Laws were codified to regulate banking operations and the first mention of such laws was written in the ancient Code of Hamarabi (circa 1760 B.C.).

In local areas where storage facilities were recognized, credit receipts from these businesses were accepted by locals as payment for third party debts. This form of transaction provided more safety because valuables were not vulnerable to robbers and greatly facilitated local trade. In short order, it became evident that cumbersome and easily falsified clay credit receipts needed to be replaced and storage facilities owners began to use grain deposits for collateral on which a common local currency of exchange could be issued in lieu of the commodity being stored. In this way, money, credit and banking began their long, close relationship. Farmer Abraham could go to his local grain storage company and borrow the locally accepted form of money issued against his grain deposits as payment on a debt or purchase. The person or merchant paid with the money knew that other locals would also accept the receipt-backed money as payment. It wasn't so much the supposed grain stored but the actual perceived value of the receipt.

As civilization expanded and empires absorbed new tribes, royal families acting as the de facto governments realized that it was beneficial and necessary to establish a currency of the realm. This local currency would facilitate the expansion of commerce and impose a subtle form of control on all subjects. Neighboring tribes who weren't part of the empire found it difficult to trade with the empire without access to the empire's currency. On the other hand, citizens of the empire found it much easier to trade within the empire. As a result, an empire's particular form of money (currency) took on an importance similar to a common language in its ability to help unite and facilitate the common good.

As discussed earlier in section 1.6, goldsmiths and jewelers had evolved into bankers and issued their own deposit receipts to clients. This practice grew rapidly as jewelers and goldsmiths discovered that they could issue more deposit receipts than they had in actual deposits. They also started to charge interest on the deposit receipts and these primordial bankers discovered a form of the "Fractional Reserve System" in that the goldsmiths and jewelers had security for only a portion of the deposit receipts that they gave out. They rationalized that the probability that all the clients would want to draw out their secure deposits of gold and jewels at the same time was highly unlikely. The fledgling bankers were literally creating assets out of nothing and creating real profits by charging interest on the ersatz receipts. This model for profitability spawned money lending in even the smallest communities. As the new banking industry spread, so did prosperity. It became delightfully obvious that the more money that was available to the population the more commerce prospered. As the new banking industry grew, so did its **political power**.

King Henry I of England decided to wrestle the power away from the goldsmith-jeweler- bank community and around 1100 A.D. he brought banking under the control of the royal central government. Moreover, the self-enlightened king decided to help control the flood of money coming into being by making the private banks match what they lent to the public by giving an equal amount to the government for the purposes of the common good. To provide for paying the interest on the public loans from the private banks, the government imposed a direct tax on all the citizens. This system lasted 726 years until 1826.

In the 18th century, the same sort of free market atmosphere allowed the banking industry in the fledgling United States to help spur rapid investment and growth. Several attempts were made to have a central bank to help regulate the amount of money being circulated (Europe had experienced several booms, busts and inflationary periods), but politics and local bankers made the attempts anemic at best. However, in 1913, the Federal Reserve Banking Act was passed in Congress and the U.S. banking system became much more regulated.

2.1 THE FRACTIONAL RESERVE SYSTEM

Gold, silver, furs or tobacco leaves, by themselves, are not "money" in the strict sense of the word. Objects become money only when they are generally accepted as symbols representing a certain amount of goods and services and thus readily accepted in exchange for other goods and services of commensurate perceived value. But as money moved from commodity backing to confidence backing, who was to make sure that the confidence and unit value stayed intact? This task became one of the most important for governments to undertake. After all, history has shown that without a stable currency a nation's ability to sustain its commerce and social cohesion can be greatly impaired.

A system to act as a conduit and control for the flow of the supply of money is essential for any modern economy. First, there needs to be a way to create a continuous supply of money and a need to establish the cost of money to help regulate the demand; seemingly simple objectives but with numerous devils in the details.

As the fathers of modern banking discovered from the gold bankers of the 17th century, more money can be issued than actually is on deposit and interest can be earned on the "phantom assets." They also learned that the same factors of supply and demand could affect the interest rates that could be charged for lending. The question then became how much money based on unbacked deposits could be loaned out. Over time, agreements were made within the local banking communities as to what percentage of deposits could be lent out. For example, banks might agree to only lend out 150% of the money they have on deposit. This ability to lend out more than is on deposit was the beginnings of the "fractional reserve system." Not only could the bankers "make money" from issuing paper but they could also "control" the supply of money and try to balance it with demand so as to allow an acceptable rate of interest to be charged on loans without killing lending activities. Of course, as there was no policing body to enforce the self-imposed restrictions, many banks looked after their own interests first and as a result, local prices (inflation) and interest rates charged for borrowing money varied from region to region.

To help stabilize prices and interest rates in the United States, Congress passed the Federal Reserve Bank Act in 1913. The purpose of the act was "to provide for the establishment of Federal reserve banks, to furnish an elastic currency, to afford means of rediscounting commercial paper, to establish a more effective supervision of banking in the United States, and for other purposes." We will address the function of the Federal Reserve Banking system in later sections.

2.2 WHAT IS A BANK?

According to Britannica, "a bank is an institution that deals in money and its substitutes and provides other financial services. Banks accept deposits and make loans and derive a profit from the difference in the interest rates paid and charged, respectively."

The primary function of banks is to put their account holders' money to use by lending it out to others who can then use it to buy homes, businesses, send kids to college, etc. Moreover, with the repeal of the Glass-Steagal Act in 1999, the wall between banks and most other forms of financial investments was removed and banks now offer clients a wide range of financial products such as mutual funds, insurance, brokering stocks, bonds and derivatives. Without doubt, banks are a critical component in the economy not only for the sale and service of financial instruments but also as the major distributors of the money supply.

2.3 HOW BANKS CREATE MONEY

When a client deposits money in a bank, the account is credited with the amount of the deposit. When a client writes checks or makes withdrawals, that amount is deducted from the client's account balance. If the client has an interest bearing account, earned interest is added to the account balance and any bank charges are deducted from the account. Not too exciting. But banks are the starting point for the magic (some consider it the devil's work) of the fractional reserve concept. In affect, banks create money. They do it by taking deposits and multiplying them many times over. How do they do that?

One of the most important tasks of The Federal Reserve Bank's Board of Governors is establishing the "reserve requirement," which is the amount of currency that a bank must have on hand or on deposit at a Federal Reserve Bank. For example, if today's reserve requirement is 3%-10%, that means that a bank with $100 million in deposits "on the books" is required to keep only $3 million to $10 million in its vaults or on deposit with a Federal Reserve bank. In our example, the bank would have a balance of deposits of $97-$90 million after the reserve requirement is placed aside. This amount could then be used to start a process that would eventually inject over a billion dollars in new funds into the economy!

Perhaps the following example will make it easier to understand how the fractional reserve concept creates money. Suppose a bank gets a new deposit of $100, then, assuming a reserve requirement of 10%, the bank can then lend out 90% of the deposit or $90. That $90 goes back into the economy to purchase goods and services and will eventually end up back in another bank as a deposit. That bank, in turn, can now lend out $81 of the new $90 deposit (the bank is required to keep $9 as its reserve requirement) and the process goes on thousands of times – all based on the original $100 deposit. In this way, the fractional reserve concept acts as a huge multiplier effect on the amount of currency put into circulation. To keep up with the continuous growth of the money supply, the Federal Reserve Bank is also charged with the responsibility of coordinating with the Department of the Treasury to make sure that enough paper money is printed to meet the needs for the myriad transactions created. Some would call it a Ponzi scheme but most others call it the genius of our modern banking system.

Figure 1: Fractional Reserve of 10%

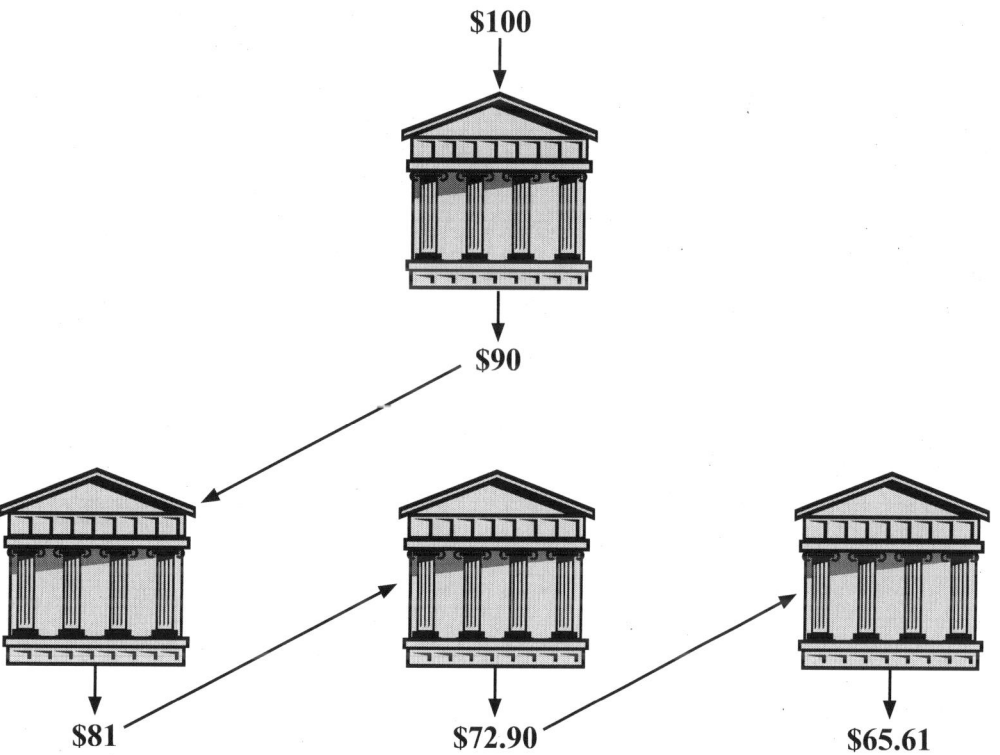

And on and on it goes!

Why Does It Work?

Over 80% of the U.S. GDP (gross domestic product) is generated by consumerism. With the advent of credit, consumers switched from a process of earning the money before making a purchase to making the purchase and then paying for it over time (with additional interest charges). Deferred gratification with all its discipline and sacrifice gave way to impulse buying and instant gratification. Some bemoan the "good old days of fiscal responsibility" but perhaps few would be willing to return if given the chance. Demand for goods and services, combined with credit, has provided high levels of employment and a general standard of living unseen in human history. Money and credit have become an essential nutrient for the growth of western civilization and recent history of just the past few years has shown that fractional reserves and accessible credit has been a major factor in helping to raise employment and standards of living in the "emerging countries," which up until recently had limited credit only for a few citizens or companies.

But for fractional reserves to work, many political-economic policies and procedures need to be kept in balance. For instance, monitoring money supply, velocity and inflationary indicators helps determine what the Federal Reserve Bank's Board of Governors decide the reserve requirement and interest rates should be. Constant monitoring of the economy and fiscal (i.e., government budgets and spending) and monetary policies (i.e., Fed interest rates and reserve requirement) is essential to keep an economy producing enough employment with little or no inflation (decreasing value of money).

Perhaps the greatest fear posed by the money supply and interest rates being decided through a partially political process is a collapse of confidence in money and credit. Dollars created by the fractional reserve concept have no value in themselves. When the gold standard was in effect, a paper dollar could be exchanged for a certain amount of gold; the dollar was backed by a tangible commodity. Today, money is just a digital entry and its value a measure of confidence in the financial system.

3.0 The Contemporary World Financial System

The world's financial system has undergone rapid and complex changes over the past few decades. Riding the wave of technology, the system has adapted nicely to keep pace with the torrid pace of global integration and the increasing creation of wealth. However, the growing complexity and interdependence among components of the system has caused some to raise a red flag of concern. Could the system crash as the result of one failing component causing a snowball effect and bringing the whole system down?

Is the lack of consistent oversight across borders making it easier for the potential fatal flaw that throws a wrench into the system and brings economic chaos? Regardless of these concerns, the system is in motion and working rather well; however, the concerns need to be addressed to ensure that the world's growing interdependent economies can continue to grow and improve the lives of billions of citizens who have yet to participate in the marvels of what the system has produced for industrialized countries. As the "emerging markets" bring more and more people into the system, the need to improve oversight and "failsafe mechanisms" will no doubt be a top priority for government regulators and leaders of the private sector.

3.1 COMPONENTS OF THE CONTEMPORARY FINANCIAL SYSTEM

The main players in the world financial system are not just national institutions but also the global institutions, such as The International Monetary Fund, the Bank for International Settlements, the World Bank, Central banks, private institutions acting on the global scale (Transnationals), Government Special Entities (GSEs) and Stock and Commodity exchanges and managed investment funds.

3.2 THE INTERNATIONAL MONETARY FUND (IMF)

Over the past decades, some confusion and erroneous statements have been made about the IMF. Before the great loan default period of the 1970's, the IMF was mainly identified with helping poorer nations obtain financing to help stimulate growth and build necessary infrastructure. Almost everybody who thought of the IMF thought of an institution dedicated to doing "missionary work" and acting as the benefactor for the poor.

However, after the world wide economic crisis spawned by the collusion of the Organization of Oil Exporting Countries (OPEC), many poorer nations couldn't meet the loan obligations needed to service the loans – not hand outs – made through the IMF. Not only did nations tell the IMF that they couldn't pay for the loan servicing, but many countries told the IMF that they *wouldn't pay the loans back*.

The IMF was immediately put into the place of acting as the "bad guy" when they acted as the intermediary between lending nations and borrowing nations. In reality, the IMF does not make the loans directly but serves as an entity that acts on behalf of its member countries. The debt crisis became a problem between member nations and the IMF was dragged in to act as arbitrator between lending and borrowing members. It became the villain when borrowing member governments had to comply with agreed-to debt terms that put hardship on the local populace. It was politically convenient to blame the economic austerity on that mean old IMF.

Contrary to popular belief, the IMF has no authority over its members. What authority the IMF does possess is confined to requiring the member nation to disclose information on its monetary and fiscal policies and to avoid problems that could affect the exchange rates of international currencies. For instance, a country can artificially devalue its currency in respect to competing countries in order to make its exports more price competitive. Moreover, the IMF helps to coordinate with other national central banks to help integrate national and international monetary policies.

Fortunately, widespread convertibility now permits easy exchange between most of the world's major currencies. Convertibility has allowed virtually unrestricted travel, trade, and investment during the past quarter of a century and has resulted largely from the cooperation of member nations with the IMF in eliminating restrictions on buying and selling national currencies.

How the IMF Functions

Member nations of the IMF are required to pay quotas to help create a pool of funds for operations and lending. However, the IMF has created its own local currency called the SDR (Special Drawing Rights). The SDRs are used for internal accounting and allocated to members by a formula based on economic factors that acts very similar to a form of security for loans made to member countries.

The IMF also reviews how countries are establishing their exchange rates and how nations "peg" their currencies to the value of a larger economy. For example, if a smaller nation pegs its currency to the currency of a larger nation, the IMF needs to advise member countries if the pegged currency is being properly adjusted. Exporting countries derive a competitive advantage if their currency is less expensive because the price of comparable goods will be less on the world market. The IMF attempts to monitor this to ensure that the foreign currency field is as level as possible. But, the IMF has no regulatory powers. It can only consult and recommend to its membership of about 186 nations.

Today, the IMF is an important private institution that helps coordinate economic issues among its global membership to facilitate trade and development. It is also a lender to its membership in cases of emergency loans. Most importantly, the IMF acts as a platform for communication on the increasingly complex issues of globalization and how to resolve present and potential conflicts.

3.3 BANK OF INTERNATIONAL SETTLEMENTS (BIS)

The Bank for International Settlements (BIS) is the world's oldest financial international organization (established in 1930), which fosters international monetary and financial cooperation and serves as a *bank for central banks*. The principal offices are in Basel, Switzerland. As its customers are central banks and international organizations, the BIS does not accept deposits from, or provide financial services to, private individuals or corporate entities. SDRs are the monetary unit used by the Bank.

The BIS was designed to act as an objective third party to help central banks and national governments better manage internal economic policy with the view of better management of international reserves (the assets denominated in foreign currency, plus gold, held by central banks).

The BIS is a specialty organization that specifically attends to central banks and provides management recommendations for how central banks can best invest and manage their assets. In other words, the BIS acts like a private money management firm for central banks.

Like most of the international institutions that make up an important part of the world's financial system, the BIS is owned by its members – the central banks. Exactly what responsibilities and accountabilities are assigned to the BIS is not clearly spelled out.

3.4 THE WORLD BANK

The World Bank describes itself as a vital source of financial and technical assistance to developing countries around the world. They are not a bank in the common sense but are made up of two unique development institutions owned by 185 member countries – the International Bank for Reconstruction and Development (IBRD) and the International Development Association (IDA).

Each institution plays a different but supportive role in our mission of reducing global poverty and the improvement of living standards. The IBRD focuses on middle income and creditworthy poor countries, while IDA focuses on the poorest countries in the world. Together they provide low-interest loans, interest-free credits and grants to developing countries for projects concerned with education, health, infrastructure, communications and many other projects that will have broad social impact.

The World Bank has a clearly defined agenda called the Millennium Development Goals, which call for the elimination of poverty and encourage sustained economic development. Specifically, the Millennium Development Goals are:

- Eradicate extreme poverty and hunger
- Achieve universal primary education
- Promote gender equality and empower women
- Reduce child mortality

- Improve maternal health
- Combat HIV/AIDS and other diseases
- Ensure environmental sustainability
- Create global partnership for development

3.5 CENTRAL BANKS -THE U.S. FEDERAL RESERVE BANK SYSTEM

We will confine this discussion to the Central Bank of the United States – The Federal Reserve Banking System. Most central banks of other nations have similar functions but with some minor differences.

The Federal Reserve System in the U.S., often referred to as the Federal Reserve or simply "the Fed," is the central bank of the United States. It was created in 1913 by Congress to provide the nation with a safer, more flexible, and more stable monetary and financial system. Over the years, its role has evolved and expanded. The Federal Reserve's responsibilities fall into four general areas:

- Conducting the nation's monetary policy by influencing money and credit conditions in the economy in pursuit of full employment and stable prices
- Supervising and regulating banking institutions to promote the safety and soundness of the nation's banking and financial system and to protect the credit rights of consumers
- Maintaining the stability of the financial system and containing systemic risk that may arise in financial markets
- Providing certain financial services to the U.S. government, to the public, to financial institutions, and to foreign official institutions, including playing a major role in operating the nation's payments systems

Structure and Function of the Federal Reserve Banking Systems

There are 12 banks in the Federal Banking System, each located in a strategic area of the country. These regional Federal Reserve Banks share responsibility for supervising and regulating financial institutions and for providing banking services to depository institutions and to the federal government; and for ensuring that consumers receive adequate information and fair treatment in their relations with the banking system. The Fed's most important operational role is raising and lowering interest rates, creating money and using a few other tools to help stimulate or slow down the economy. This manipulation is aimed at maintaining low inflation, high employment rates, and targeted economic output. More on how the Fed actually manipulates the economy will be discussed in Section 3.

The Federal Reserve Bank is considered an *independent* central bank because its decisions do not have to be ratified by the President or anyone else in the executive or legislative branch of government. Moreover, the Fed does not receive funding from Congress, and the terms of the members of the Board of Governors can span multiple presidential and congressional terms; this supposedly precludes the possibility of a political appointee being put at the head of one of the most powerful financial institutions in the world. However, the Federal Reserve is subject to oversight by Congress, which periodically reviews its activities and can alter its responsibilities by statute. The main idea of keeping the bank as free from politics as possible is that the Central Bank wields considerable power to influence the economy and thus the socio-political state of the nation with ramifications for the rest of the world. For example, if an incumbent president wants to be re-elected, "convincing" (jawboning) the Central Bank to stimulate the economy might be good for the incumbent but eventually not for the country (spurring the potential for inflation). Responsibility for the proper management of a large part of the U.S. banking system along with controlling interest rates and money supply rests on the broad shoulders of the Federal Reserve Bank.

Ownership of the Fed

There exists some confusion on exactly who owns the Fed. It certainly sounds like a federal institution but such is not the case. Congress does have oversight of the Fed but the Fed is owned by member banks – which are privately owned. The Reserve Banks issue shares of stock to member banks. However, because of restrictions, owning stock in the Reserve Bank is quite different from owning stock in a private company. The Reserve Banks are not operated for profit, and ownership of a certain amount of stock is, by law, a condition of membership in the Federal Reserve System. The stock of the Fed may not be sold, traded, or pledged as security for a loan; dividends are, by law, limited to 6 percent per year.

The Federal Reserve's income is derived primarily from the interest on U.S. government securities that it has acquired through open market operations. Other sources of income are the interest on foreign currency investments held by the System, fees received for services provided to depository institutions, such as check clearing, funds transfers, and automated clearinghouse operations; and interest on loans to depository institutions. After paying its expenses, the Federal Reserve turns the rest of its earnings over to the U.S. Treasury. Because of the protection of secrecy, the Fed is not required to file any sort of written financial report and nobody seems to know exactly what the real financial status of Fed operations are.

The President of the United States appoints the Chairman of the Fed for a four-year term which can be repeated without term limit. The chairman, along with the Federal Open Market Committee (FOMC), which is made up of other regional Fed bank presidents, oversees open market operations, the main tool used by the Federal Reserve to influence money market conditions and the growth of money and credit mainly through controlling interest rates and reserve requirements.

3.6 INVESTMENT BANKS AND COMMERCIAL BANKS

Investment banks are different from Commercial banks. The main reason for this is that investment banks are not financial intermediaries in the sense that they do not take deposits and lend them out. They focus on assisting new and established corporations in the issuance of securities (equity financing), mergers and acquisitions and leveraged buyouts (LBOs). Investment banks play a major role in obtaining equity financing for public and private companies and local and federal governments. They receive fees for their service instead of interest payments on loans, as do commercial banks. Investment Banks help corporations meet SEC (Securities and Exchange Commission) regulations, and due diligence requirements for public funding. In other words, Investment banks act as catalysts in helping corporations transform themselves through obtaining private or public financing. They make their income on a deal-by-deal basis and risk is limited as a result. Governments also turn to investment banks to help issue bonds when they need financing from the public for projects such as the construction of schools, roads, sewers, and other public works that aren't funded by tax revenues.

Commercial banks, on the other hand, are focused on the needs of individuals and businesses. They offer a wide range of financial services to the public and function as distribution points for the nation's money supply. Commercial banks (including almost all types of retail banks) make profits mainly from lending depositor funds to clients and collecting interest on the loans. As many loans are longer term, the bank is greatly concerned about default risk since loans are subject to the changes in the economy and each individual payer's life and the ability to pay during economic cycles. These banks will only receive profit if enough borrowers can meet their loan obligations. Both commercial and investment banks are key players in the economy and making sure they are operated with the highest moral and professional capacity is essential for the economic health of the nation. This fact holds true for most of the industrialized western economies.

3.7 GOVERNMENT SPONSORED ENTITIES (GSES)

Government sponsored enterprises (GSEs) are a group of hybrid financial services corporations created by the United States Congress. Their function is to reduce interest rates for specific borrowing sectors of the economy such as for students, farmers, and homeowners. The government backs the GSE companies through guarantees against insolvency and the GSEs act as loan qualification and administration agents. Additionally, the GSEs *securitize loans* and move them into the arena of public finance.

Securitization is the packaging of pools of loans or receivables for redistribution to investors. Investors buy the repackaged assets in the form of securities (shares of stock) which are collateralized (secured) on the underlying pool and its associated income stream. *Securitization thereby converts illiquid assets into liquid assets.* Examples of GSEs include: Federal Home Loan Bank, Federal Home Loan Mortgage Corporation (Freddie Mac), Federal Farm Credit Bank, Resolution Funding Corporation and the Government National Mortgage Association (Ginnie Mae). The two largest housing GSEs, Fannie Mae (FNMA), and Freddie Mac (FMAC) own and/or securitize approximately of 70% of all the residential mortgage loans in the United States.

One of the problems with securitizing loans is that loans with good credit backing are bundled with other loans of lower quality but the investor who purchases shares of the packaged mortgages doesn't know this fact. If there are defaults on the underlying mortgages, income for the GSE will be effected and can greatly effect the price of the stock purchased by the investor. So, as an investor, this type of *derivative investment* may not have the measure of transparency needed to make the best investing decisions.

3.8 STOCK, FOREIGN EXCHANGE (FOREX) AND COMMODITY EXCHANGES

The function of all market exchanges is to facilitate matching seller and buyer and seeing to the clearing of the transaction. There are over twenty large stock markets throughout the world and hundreds of smaller ones in almost every country in the world. There are twenty-seven commodity exchanges worldwide and the ubiquitous Foreign Exchange market (FOREX) is by far the largest financial market of them all.

Stock and Bond Markets

To raise cash, a *public company* has several alternatives: 1) it can borrow money from a bank and pay principal and interest payments over a specific time; 2) a company may sell bonds to the public to raise cash; however, the company must pay interest – usually at lower rates than can be obtained by borrowing from a bank; 3) it can raise money by offering shares of ownership in the company. This is called *equity financing* and entails no interest charges to the company and creates little or no long term financial liabilities. Basically, the companies sell small pieces of ownership for cash. The investor plans to make money on the increasing value of the company as represented in the price of a share of the company.

Typically, when a private company has grown to a certain size with good profits and a good story, management of the privately owned company may opt to look for financing its growth and moving "to the next level" by offering ownership to the public. To do this, the company must go through a long and expensive process to be able to qualify to sell shares to the public on a public stock exchange. In the Unites States, the Security and Exchange Commission (SEC) is responsible for making sure new companies meet all the requirements of transparency and financial verification and also that the sales practices and procedures of public companies are in compliance with rules and regulations as specified by the SEC. Investment banks help bring the new companies to the public in what is called an initial public offering (IPO). Once a company becomes a public company, management is controlled by a Board of Directors elected by the stockholders. The Board of Directors is responsible for representing the interests of stock holders and oversees the hiring and operations of the top level management team.

Commodities Exchanges

Generally, commodities are basic resources such as agricultural products, iron ore, steel, coal, gasoline, ethanol, sugar, soybeans, coffee, aluminum, pork bellies, rice, wheat, gold, diamonds, silver and many other products. The commodity exchanges (23 worldwide) allow the total marketplace to set prices and allow sellers and buyers to have an idea of demand and adjust supply accordingly. It's a carefully choreographed economic dance with price and supply being dictated by the music of the market place. The commodity exchanges also make sure that the proper product is delivered and acts as a clearing agent for sellers and buyers. The Commodities Exchanges trade more than ten times the total value of all the world's stock markets on any given day.

The commodity exchanges help to keep commodity prices lower by allowing users of the commodities the ability to purchase futures contracts, which guarantee delivery at a future date at a specific price. This type of transaction helps reduce risks of supply and demand dislocations and, in the end, benefits all consumers who directly or indirectly use the major commodities.

The Foreign Exchange Market (FOREX)

Major currencies are traded by governments, businesses and speculators to the tune of about $2 *trillion* per day. Most of the major currencies are floating (not fixed) and change value in respect to each other at any given moment in time. As in the case of commodities exchanges (currencies are also a commodity), traders buy and sell currencies based on the free and transparent (as much as possible) flow of information. In this way, the value of a nation's currency is set by the consensus of what the market dictates on a second-by-second basis.

Also as in commodities exchanges, the FOREX also offers futures contracts. A currency future contract has great practicality for international trade. For example, if a distributor in the U.S. who imports Japanese radios will be receiving a shipment in three months, he may want to purchase a future Japanese Yen contract for the amount to cover the purchase price of the order. He would do this if he felt that the US currency might devalue (become cheaper) against the Japanese Yen. If this happens, the distributor would have to pay more in US dollars at the higher exchange rate when the order arrives. A future contract will allow the holder to take advantage of a price movement and pocket the profit to make up the difference between the two currencies. On the other hand, if the distributor believes that the Japanese Yen will go down in relation to the US dollar, the importer's dollars will be exchanged at the higher rate when the order arrives and the distributor would be purchasing the delivery at a lower U.S. dollar price.

Example: U.S. importer orders $10,000 USD for 50 new Sony short wave radios. The radios are scheduled for shipment from Tokyo in 3 months. As the Japanese manufacturer is located in Japan, it prefers to take payment in Japanese Yen. At the time of the order, the U.S. dollar can purchase 116 Yen. Therefore, today, the order is valued at 1,160,000 Yen equivalent to $10,000 USD.

The importer does some research and finds out that currency traders expect the dollar to devalue against the yen, which means that in the future, the dollar will purchase fewer yen and the future price of the order will increase in terms of dollars. As a result, the importer purchases a "mini future contract" for US dollar-Japanese yen. The importer sells the dollar short, meaning that he believes that the dollar will go down in value and if that does happen, his future contract will increase in value and would yield a profit. There are no commission charges or other transaction fees to purchase a future contract.

Three months later when the order has landed in the U.S., the dollar can now only purchase 113 yen. That means that the price for the 50 short wave radios in U.S. dollars is now $10,175.44 (1,160,000 yen/114 yen per dollar) – a price increase of $175.44. However, the Dollar-Yen contract gained about $300 in value. The importer closes out his USD/Yen contract and pockets the $300 profit. The importer made more than enough to pay for the decrease in the exchange rate. If the importer had believed that the value of the U.S. dollars would go up vis-à-vis the yen, he would not need to purchase a future contract because when the order arrived, the U.S. dollar would be stronger (could buy more yen) and the original price of $10,000 would be less because it would take fewer dollars to buy the 1,1650,00 yen to cover the delivery.

Private Investment Funds and Hedge Funds

Mutual funds are pooled funds that are professionally managed to optimize returns on a flexible investment portfolio. The advantage of mutual funds is that they allow investors the ability to purchase a variety of stocks and bonds with lower amounts of investment capital. This happens because the pooled funds can purchase the stocks of companies and then divide portions of shares among the fund investors. For example: if an investor had only $2,000 to invest, instead of buying just a few individual shares, the investor can buy shares of a mutual fund that already owns a large and varied portfolio of companies. This low cost diversification of investments reduces risk and can provide the small investor with professional management and supposedly better returns than more conservative investments like savings accounts, money markets and certificates of deposit.

Most IRAs and 401(K) pension plans invest heavily in mutual funds. Many American workers have their "nest egg" in mutual funds. The Investment Company Institute (ICI) estimated in 2006 that in the USA alone mutual funds represent over $9.7 trillion. Keeping in mind that mutual funds invest mainly in stocks and bonds, they provide a huge pool of no or low interest funding for public companies and governments, which should help reduce corporate borrowing costs and increase corporate profits. Ideally, more profits mean more jobs.

Hedge Funds

The number of hedge funds increased 10% during the past year to reach around 9,000 with an estimated $1.2 trillion under management. Hedge funds are considered risky and are usually used by wealthy and sophisticated investors. Hedge funds invest in a variety of investment vehicles and not just conventional stocks bonds and mutual funds. They look for investments to help add diversification and high profit potential. One of the most interesting things about Hedge funds is that a portion of their portfolios are targeted to perform in adverse market conditions. If the markets turn ugly, there are always some investments and techniques to take advantage of a negative situation. Because of the high risk-return and the fact that many fund managers get most of their income from profits generated by the fund, some of the best money managers and financial analysts are in the Hedge Fund industry. In 2006, *the top 25 hedge fund managers earned an average of $440 million for a total of $15 billion in total compensation!* The funds themselves matched returns of the general stock markets but it's their counter market orientation that can bring superior results in times of instability – or so the sales pitch goes.

3.9 SOME CONCERNS

Some regulators have voiced concern that all of these complex and interconnected components of today's modern financial system might have a built-in vulnerability. If, for some reason, there is an unwinding of the financial system, it could cause a domino effect and wreak havoc on many of the world's economies. In the U.S. alone, bank consolidation has seen the top five domestic bank holding companies now in possession of about 45 percent of all banking assets, almost twice the share as they had just 20 years ago. Also, there are only two institutions that clear financial transactions worth over $2 trillion each day! What would happen if one of these companies shuts down? The interaction of all financial activities depends on a huge, interconnected and complex technological infrastructure with its own peculiar vulnerabilities. But the good news is that regulators and institutional leaders are very aware of the potential weaknesses and they are constantly looking for ways to improve and protect the world's critical financial system.

 4.0 The Role of Interest Rates

Basically, interest rates are the cost of borrowing money. The interest rate charged is a function of several factors, the most important of which are: loan risk and inflation. Risk refers more to the circumstances of the loan, such as qualifications of the borrower, the nature of the loan and term of the loan, etc. Inflation is the constant devaluation of currency.

Inflation

Inflation is the erosion of the value of money over time. There are many definitions of inflation but in general, it's the general upward price movement of goods and services in an economy, usually as measured by the Consumer Price Index (CPI) and the Producer Price Index (PPI). The Producer Price Index (PPI) measures what is happening to the cost end of the buying channel. If costs of production increase, it will eventually be passed on to the consumption end or absorbed because of competitive pressures. The Consumer Price Index measures what is happening on the consumption end of the buying channel. If demand is increasing retail prices, it will be demonstrated by the fact that PPI doesn't rise, but CPI does. This may indicate a shortage of goods and services or excess demand. Inflation is indicated by both PPI and CPI. For example, if the cost of steel goes up because of strong demand, the PPI will go up. This is called *cost driven inflation*. The cost of a stove to a distributor may go up because of the added cost of steel but competitive pricing and existing inventory might keep the retail price the same. If the distributor can't increase retail price because of competition, the margin of profit is decreased for the distributor. One of the advantages of a more global economy is there is more competition, which can provide more mitigation on prices even though PPI may be increasing.

On the other hand, if there is an excess demand for a good or service that allows retailers to ask and get a higher price, this is called *demand driven inflation*. The Fed keeps a very close eye on CPI and PPI as indicators of inflation. Normally, indications of rising inflation will prompt a rise in interest rates in an attempt to cool down the economy and reduce demand by making money more expensive to borrow. Usually, the Fed will use small incremental increases or decreases in interest rates (usually Fed Funds rate) to help "tweak" demand and supply.

4.1 EFFECTS OF INFLATION

If, for example, the inflation rate is forecast to be 3% over the next ten years, $100 today will be worth **$78.14 ten years from now. Another way to look at it is what costs $100 today will cost $127.98 ten years from now – provided that inflation**

stays constant at 3%. If you are a lender, you don't want to lose the value of the money you've lent. So lenders are very aware of what the forecasts for inflation are. Lenders need to first consider what interest rate will compensate for the erosion of loan principal caused by inflation and then add an additional amount of interest to provide a positive return over and above the inflation rate and costs of servicing the loan. In other words, the profitability of a loan and the interest to be charged will depend on forecasts for inflation, risk factors such as borrower qualifications, type of loan and costs of servicing the loan. Once the cumulative interest rate is figured out, it will usually have a little margin for adjustment to match the competition – if the potential borrower pushes the issue and the bank wants the loan.

Example:
- Loan amount: $100,000 for 20 years
- Average inflation forecast for 20 years: 3%
- Loan administrative and other costs: .5 %
- Profit target: 6%
- Interest rate to be charged: 9.5%

4.2 TIME VALUE OF MONEY

Because of the ravages of inflation, many investors want to know how much money must be invested today at a certain interest rate to provide a certain amount over time. A good example would be when saving for a child's education. If future tuition and books are estimated to cost $200,000 for four years of university twelve years from now when your child is ready to go to college, a person can calculate how much needs to be invested today to yield the $200,000 by the time your child is ready for college. This is called *present value of money*.

Example of Present Value

If you have $10,000 today, what will that be worth in the future? In other words, to find the *present value* of the future $10,000, we need to find out how much we would have to invest today at a certain interest rate to receive the equivalent of $10,000 in the future.

Formula for finding Present Value is: $PV = (FV) * (1+i)^{-n}$

PV= Present Value; FV= Future Value; i = interest rate; n = number of years

Example question: Let's say you can obtain a loan for an interest rate of 4.5 % for 1 year. What amount of money will you need to invest today to have $10,000 in one year?

1)   FV= $10,000; i= .045; n= 1
2) $10,000 * (1+.045)$^{-1}$
3)   PV= $10,000\ 1.045= $9,569

So, the *Present Value* of $10,000 one year from now is $9,569 today – if invested at 4.5%

However, if the inflation rate is 3% over the one years, the *real return* will only be 1.5% which would not have preserved today's $10,000. Therefore, it is important to adjust the formula interest rate for estimated inflation.

1)   FV= $10,000; i= .015* n=1
2) $10,000 * (1+.015)$^{-1}$
3)   PV= $10,000\ 1.015= $9,852.22

Therefore at a 4.5% interest rate per year and an estimated inflation rate of 3% per year, you would need to invest $9,852.22 (present value) today to have $10,000 *real dollars* in one year.

* 4.5% rate less estimated inflation rate of 3%;

Future Value

Typically, most investors want to know what would be the return on an investment made over a certain period of time at a certain interest rate. Computing this value is called *future value*.

Example: If you have $10,000 to invest today at 4.5 % for 10 years, what would be the total value of your investment 10 years from today?

Formula for finding Future Value: $FV = P * (1+i)^n$

FV= Future Value; P = Principal (Original amount); i = interest rate; n = periods

Example: You invest $10,000 for 10 years at 8% interest.

1)   FV= $10,000 * (1+.08)^{10}
2)   FV= $10,000 * (1.08)^{10} = $21,590

In 10 years at 8% annual interest rate, your original $10,000 investment would be equal to $21,560.

To find out what the inflation adjusted value would be (*real dollars*), you would subtract the estimated annual inflation from the annual interest rate for a net interest rate. For example, if inflation is estimated to be at 3% for the 10-year period in the above example, the net interest rate would be 5% (8%-3%). In which case an inflation adjusted return would be:

1) $FV = \$10,000 * (1+.05)^{10} = \$16,290$ adjusted for inflation

Your $10,000 investment would purchase $16,290 worth of goods or services 10 years from now.

Opportunity Cost

If you hadn't invested your money at all and had just put it under your mattress, 10 years from now your $10,000 would be worth about $7,800. Therefore, it would have cost you about $8,490 over the ten years by *not investing* at the inflation-adjusted interest rate of 5% as portrayed in the above example. This loss is called the "opportunity cost." Excess funds should not stay idle because of the opportunity costs. Every government, institution, business and individual needs to be cognizant of the stealth thieves of inflation and opportunity costs.

4.3 THE INFLUENCE OF INTEREST RATES

The figure below depicts how lower interest rates can affect the economy.

Figure 2: How low interest rates affect the economy

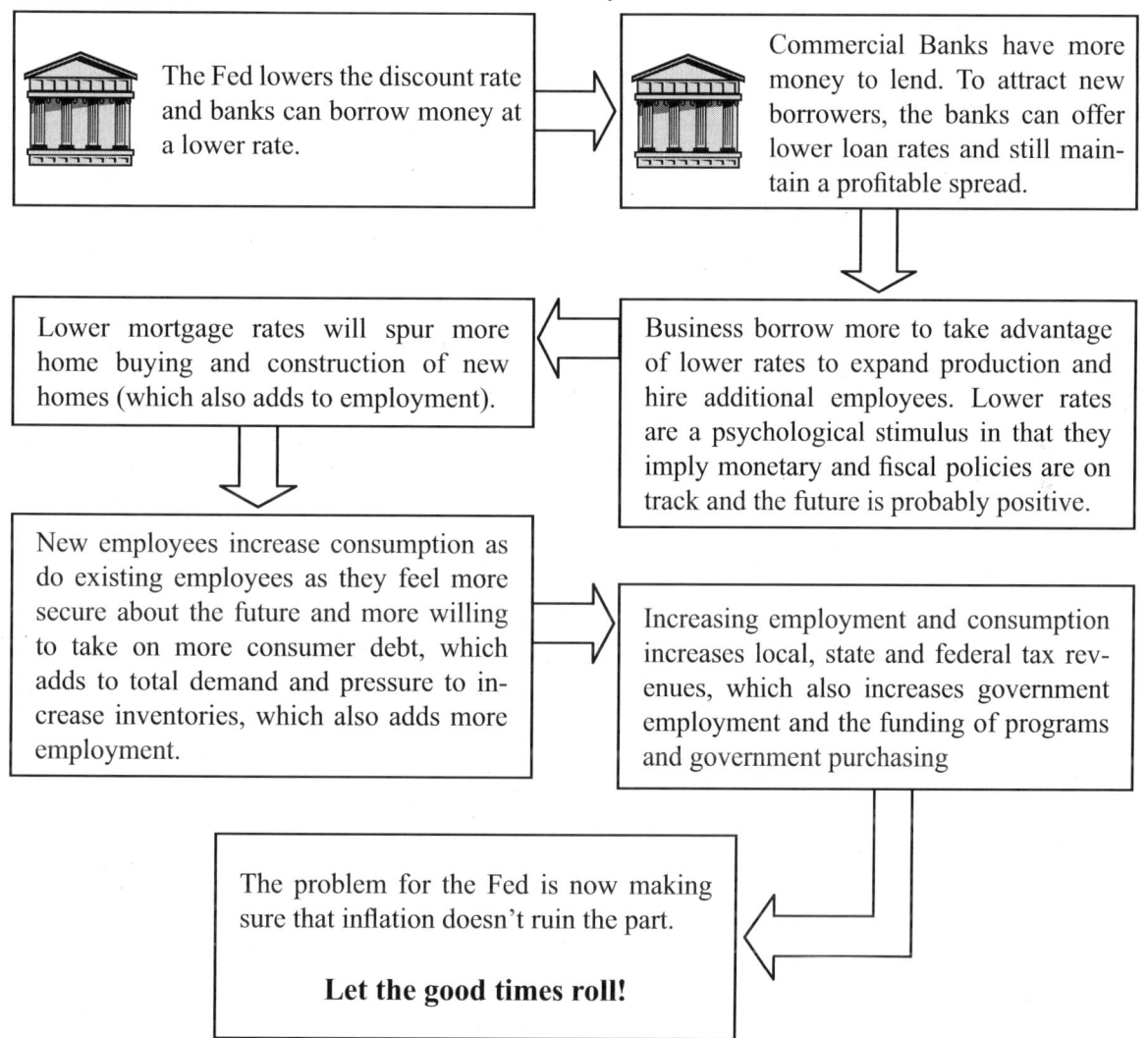

The Dark Side of Interest Rates

For the past two or more decades, the U.S. economy has been stable and many young people new to the work force haven't experienced the downside of a business cycle. The following example portrays the nightmare feared by all governments, central banks and members of society.

Most businesses and individuals need to borrow money at some time for many different reasons. Decision makers need to know how much it would cost to borrow money and if the benefits will justify the costs. If interest rates are too high, a borrower may elect to put off plans to borrow. On a more dynamic basis, if interest rates reach a level where benefits don't warrant the cost of borrowing, purchases of goods and services will decline. As purchasing declines, fewer employees are needed to produce goods and services. Businesses cut back on expansion plans. New employees that might have been needed won't be hired. Stores not only lose revenue from now unemployed workers but also the purchases that new employees might have made. The government has fewer wages to tax and government programs are cut back on hiring for lack of funding. With interest rates that don't promote growth and expansion, the economy can be greatly affected by the ripple effect. As demand decreases, businesses will reduce inventory and this will send tremors down the chain of production as more and more people lose their jobs and their ability to consume as before. If unemployment continues, the unemployed might become desperate and turn to crime to survive and the social fabric starts to unravel.

On the other hand, *if interest rates are too low* and everybody is borrowing money, the economy is in danger of "overheating." Eventually, the higher demand for goods and services will start to push prices higher as supplies become tighter and production approached full capacity. Businesses and individuals who borrowed money at a certain interest rate and used the borrowed money to invest in something else with a possibility of a higher return make investments more risky. More and more money is chasing goods and services. The increasing demand allows prices to rise until they reach a rate of increase that outpaces the perceived value and ability for income to match the rise in prices. And like a spring stretched out to its maximum length, the whole economy starts to contract as businesses and individuals slow down their purchasing and borrowing, many businesses start to see sales decline and start to lay people off their jobs. Now, there are fewer people with income to spend and the whole process starts to snowball. Homes of the newly unemployed start to flood the market and the oversupply drives prices down. As the economic contraction starts to accelerate, panic hits the public and more people decrease their purchasing habits and put homes and other personal items up for sale. The growing supply of goods for sale drives prices down even further. Soon, people can't sell homes for a price sufficient to cover the loans they borrowed from the bank. The same thing happens to auto loans. Suddenly, the banks have more and more home foreclosures and repossessed cars than they can sell. People need to tap their savings and because of the fractional reserve system, the banks don't have enough cash on hand to pay depositors. The word gets out and there's a rush to the banks to take out savings before the money runs out. Soon, many other banks have to close their doors because they have no money. Looting starts – part in anger and part in need. Government assistance for the really needy closes down because of dwindling tax revenue. Chaos sets in and law and order disappear.

Unfortunately, this scenario has been played out in the past with traumatic consequences. Because of this past history of money and banking, governments have learned the importance of the cost of borrowing money. In 1684, the first Central bank – the

Bank of England – was chartered with one of its main purposes to help regulate interest rates charged by banks. Even back then, it was clearly understood that the rates charged for borrowed funds was directly correlated with the common economic well being of the community. So, keeping interest rates within a certain range is a constant juggling act and failing to do a decent job can cause widespread misery.

4.4 THE U.S. FEDERAL RESERVE BANK AND HOW INTEREST RATES ARE DETERMINED

For the purposes of instruction, we will use the model of the U.S. banking system but most central banking systems function in a similar manner. Moreover, since World War II, the U.S. dollar has been the international currency and this makes the U.S. central bank also very influential in the international financial context.

The Role of the Federal Reserve Banking System

The "Fed's" most important function is to control inflation without causing an economic recession. The Fed has the power to regulate the economy by making the money it loans to the banking system (Fed Funds) expensive by raising interest rates or cheap by lowering rates. It can also control the amount of fractional reserves a bank must maintain in order to borrow money from the Fed. The higher the fractional reserve requirement, the less money a bank can loan. Simply put, the Fed can control interest rates and money supply. The combination of low interest rates and low fractional reserves equals an "accommodative" monetary policy. High interest rates and high fractional reserves would mean "tight" monetary policy. The rates set by the Fed also can have a major impact on the rates of return on various investments and thus can greatly affect the performance of the stock and bond markets. Moreover, interest rates can have a direct affect on currency exchange rates. There is no doubt that when the Fed speaks, the financial world listens.

4.5 THE FEDERAL FUNDS RATE AND RESERVE REQUIREMENT

Fed Funds Rate

The Federal Reserve Bank (central bank) is the bank for the banking system. It not only makes loans to member banks but also establishes at what rate other banks can lend overnight to each other – this is called the *Federal Funds rate*. If the Fed feels that the economy needs to be stimulated, it can lower the federal funds rate and this will stimulate more bank lending because banks will be able to offer lower interest rates to customers and that should stimulate borrowing.

Banks make their profits mainly by borrowing money from depositors and the Fed at a certain rate and re-loaning it to customers at a higher rate. The difference between the

Fed Funds rate and retail loan rates is called a "spread." Competition keeps the spread fairly close between banks but just as the cost of a barrel of oil eventually affects the price of everything that is made of or uses oil, a rise in the fed funds rate will affect all that is related to borrowing.

If the Fed believes that the economy is over stimulated and inflation is rising, the Fed Funds rate could be increased and thus narrow the spread between what the banks pay for money and what they can charge for it. Normally, if the cost of money becomes more expensive for the bank, it will also become more expensive for customers. When loan rates increase, borrowing usually decreases as does the amount of money in circulation. A decrease in economic growth can cause a cutback in demand and in employment. The Fed is the watchdog for the economy and tries to keep inflation, unemployment and Gross Domestic Product (GDP) in balance as much as possible and one of the main controls is through the Fed Funds rate, which indirectly controls the money supply.

Figure 3: Fed Fund rates and the Business Cycle

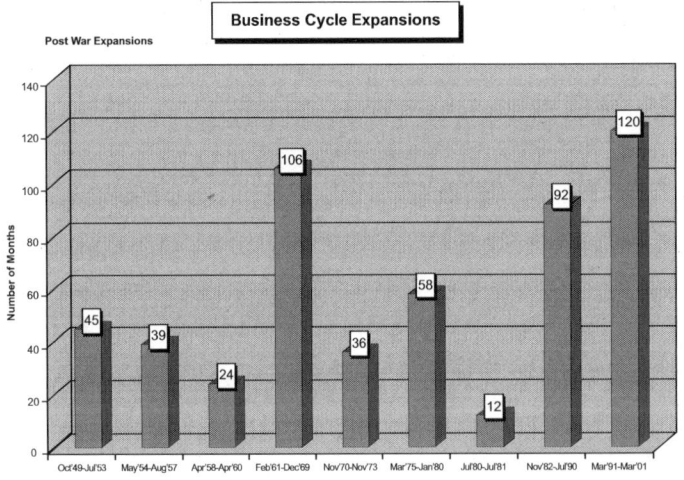

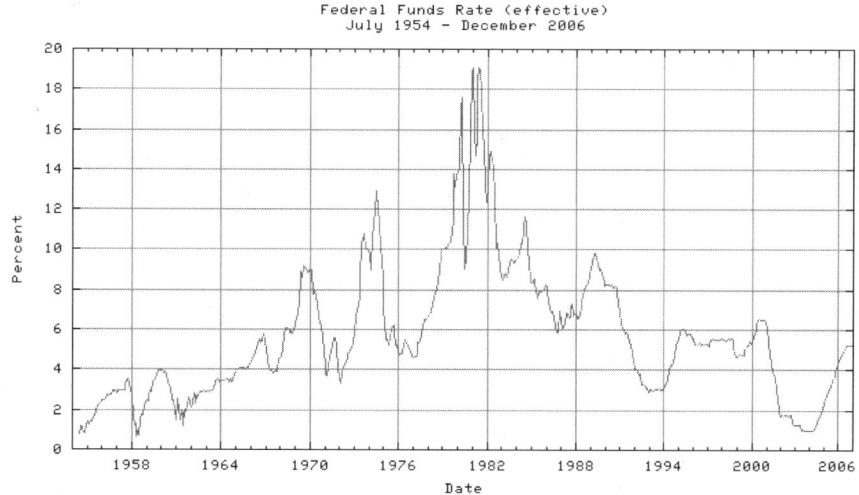

4.6 OTHER IMPORTANT TYPES OF FINANCIAL INTEREST RATES

Changes in the fed funds rate have far-reaching effects by influencing the borrowing cost of banks in the overnight lending market, and subsequently the profits on other bank products such as certificates of deposit, savings accounts, and money market accounts. If the fed funds rate is increased, the spread between what banks must pay to borrow and at what rate they can lend the funds out to borrowers is reduced. In Figure 3 above, note that during the period when the Fed funds rate was highest, the economic expansion was the smallest. This period of high fed funds rates was mainly due to the inflation caused by the two periods of Middle Eastern oil shocks (OPEC and overthrow of the Shah of Iran).

Some other more important rates, which are directly affected by changes in the Fed Fund rate, are:

Discount Rate

The rate charged by the central bank to qualified banks that make a loan *directly from the central bank*. It is distinct from the fed funds rates, which determine the rate at which banks lend money to *each other*.

Prime Rate

The Prime Interest Rate is the interest rate charged by banks to their most credit-worthy customers, usually the most prominent and stable business customers. The rate is almost always the same among major banks. In general, the prime rate runs approximately 300 basis points (3 percent) above the Fed Funds rate. Other financial instruments such as credit cards and student loans are based on the Prime rate plus an additional spread for risk and profit.

Government Bond Interest Rates

One method that the government has to obtain financing from the public is to issue bonds guaranteed by the full faith and credit of the government. Next to cash-in-hand, government bonds are considered the next safest thing. However, if the government is being run in a way that convinces investors that it isn't acting in a fiscally prudent way, the buyers of government bonds will require a higher return in the form of an interest rate paid to the holder of the bond. In this way, government bond interest rates are a vote of confidence in the monetary and fiscal policy of the issuing government.

Reserve Requirement

The Fed can also alter the reserve requirements for banks and in this way limit the amount of funds that can be lent out. When the bank is required to keep more deposits on hand rather than have the ability to lend, the reduced supply of funds available to borrowers may raise demand and thus allow the bank to raise interest rates. If the Fed decides to use the reserve requirements, it eventually has a similar effect as raising fed fund rates; however, using reserve requirement manipulation is slower in effecting the economy. As the economy is like a huge ship in motion, it takes time for changes to occur. As a result, the Federal Reserve Bank has a tendency to rely much more on using interest rate changes to affect the economy.

In the 1970s the first oil shocks hit the world and wreaked havoc with the world's financial system. The ripple effect of skyrocketing energy prices made inflation take off and the Fed had to put the clamps down hard by raising Fed Fund rates so high that the demand for commercial and retail borrowing practically disappeared. The Fed Chairman (Chairman of the Fed Board of Governors) at that difficult time was Paul Volcker and he was able to stand up (he needed all of his six-foot, seven inches) to the considerable political pressure to ease up but he stuck to the path of tight monetary policy and restraint and within a few years, most economies made the adjustment and interest rates and inflation came down. In 1989, Alan Greenspan took over as Fed Chairman and under his leadership, the U.S. and world economies have been able to have relatively stable interest rates, which has allowed for continued expansion, low inflation and improved employment for the better part of two decades.

 5.0 Banking and Indirect Finance

If you go to your rich uncle and obtain a loan from him, you have obtained *direct financing*. It's just you – the borrower, and him – the lender. If you go to a bank to obtain a loan, you deal with the bank management to ask them to lend you some of their depositors' money. The bank acts as an *intermediary* in that the bank facilitates the transaction and you don't deal directly with the depositors. This is called *indirect finance*.

5.1 HOW A BANK FUNCTIONS

Why do we deposit funds in a bank? Is it because funds are safer in a bank than keeping money in the house? Is it because we can earn interest on our deposit to help conserve some of the value of our money against inflation? Is it because we can have the convenience of checking, electronic banking and have access to cash machines on any street corner? Did you know that banks can now sell stocks, bonds, mutual funds and insurance? Banks are now one-stop shopping for most financial needs. In today's modern society, not having a bank account is usually an indication of extreme poverty, privacy concerns or obfuscation.

When we give a bank our money to keep safe for us, the bank actually turns around and gives it to someone else in order to make money for itself. How safe is that! In reality, the banks will give us a credit for the amount deposited and then use the deposit to lend out to others or pool it with other deposits and borrow from other banks to be able to make even more loans to other borrowers. Because banks can legally extend considerably more credit than they actually have in deposits, the bank becomes a major distribution point for the economy's money supply. It's a very important role and banks are literally supplying the lifeblood to the economy.

Most of us have total trust in the bank's ability to protect our money and give it to us when we ask for it. Besides, most bank accounts have federal deposit insurance to protect our deposits up to $100,000 for each account. Banks are critical to our modern economy because they function as creators of money, intermediaries for loans, provide checking, savings and other financial services. Without banks as the distribution points for money and credit, maintaining a vibrant economy would be impossible.

As mentioned, a bank usually takes deposits and approaches the regional Federal Reserve Bank or other banks in order to use the new funds to secure even more money (10 to 13 times more than the deposits) to make more loans. As the principal way banks make money is through interest paid to them on loans to borrowers, more loans mean more interest payments, which translate into more profits. For example, if your bank takes in $200,000 in new deposits for one day, that $200,000 can be "transformed" into over a $2 million credit in favor of the bank, which can then be lent out to borrowers! What a business!

The bank makes a profit from the spread it can charge between the cost of borrowed money it pays to the fed or other banks and the interest it can charge on various types of loans. It's up to each individual bank to establish its own profit targets and make as much profit as possible but competition helps to keep the spread to a level the market will support. To make sure prudent and fair lending practices are uniformly in practice throughout the banking system, the Federal Reserve and State regulators are charged with the responsibility of ensuring banks qualify and comply with federal and state banking regulations.

The fact that banks lend out more money than they have on deposit doesn't seem to make depositors nervous. Historically, there have been "runs" on banks when bank customers feared that their money wasn't safe and when they all showed up at the bank at more or less the same time, indeed the banks didn't have enough cash on hand to pay all the customers. Customers felt that they had been robbed and their resulting angry frustration can turn to violence. That is one of the main reasons that the Federal and State regulators exist: to make sure bank runs don't happen.

Today, there are many safety mechanisms in place to make sure that the fractional reserve requirements don't leave banks and their customers high and dry if for some reason there is a run. Not only is there Federal Deposit insurance on all deposits up to $100,000 for each account (there are some restrictions), but also the entire Fed and member banks are ready to supply cash if – on rare occasions – there is a run on a member bank. The most recent run on the banking system happened as recently as 1985 when some Savings and Loan banks in the southwest suffered a large number of loan defaults on government guaranteed funding and several banks had to shut their doors. The event sent a shudder through the U.S. banking industry and fostered the fear that a massive failure of depositor trust in the banking system would trigger a nationwide run on the banking system. The Fed came to the rescue to make sure there was enough liquidity and the banking system made it through the crisis with little serious consequence.

In the U.S. and most developed economies, most citizens – even without knowing about the many regulations and protections – trust the banking institutions. In the less developed countries, however, the frequent failures of local banks have made citizens reluctant to use banks and as a result, credit is difficult to secure and economic growth greatly retarded. One might say that confidence in the political-economics of a country is directly correlated with the use of banking institutions. The fact is, without the ability to create credit to support and promote growth, only the oligopoly can afford to build businesses. As a result, economic democracy, which allows new players to develop wealth, is throttled and helps perpetuate societies with extremely concentrated wealth and power.

Trust and confidence in the socio-economic-political system is what allows the banking systems to function and flourish. If the banking system were stripped of its regulatory and insurance provisions, would you put your money in a company that lends out many times more than it takes in? Most of us do it on a daily basis without a microsecond of hesitation. Indeed, our financial system is built on trust and perception.

5.2 TYPES OF BANKS

We can make a broad differentiation of types of banks:

- Retail banking, which caters to the needs of individuals and businesses;
- Investment banking, which is concerned with financing for public companies and governments through *direct financing* with financial markets; and
- Offshore banking, which usually operates with the main intent of providing banking secrecy and less regulatory restrictions.

The *retail banking* sector used to be much more differentiated in that commercial banks were primarily established to service the needs of business clients. To offer services to individuals, other types of banks appeared such as Savings and Loans, Savings Banks and Credit Unions. However, recent years have seen the retail sector undergo a consolidation frenzy in which various banks have merged to become large multi-service institutions that provide a broad range of services and products to all sizes of businesses and individuals.

Investment banking has an important niche in assisting specific corporate and governmental needs for funding, mergers, acquisitions, leveraged buyouts (LBOs), initial public offerings (IPOs) and other more exotic investment instruments such as bonds and derivatives. Investment banks are very specialized and bridge the gap between the public financial markets and the needs for direct financing of businesses and governments.

- *Mergers and acquisition*s take place when two or more businesses decide to legally consolidate their companies and either form a new company or one of the companies maintains the corporate identity and absorbs the other. A good example is the merger of The Bank of America and Barnett Bank. The surviving company is The Bank of America and Barnett Bank was totally absorbed. Typically mergers are done to take advantage of *economies of scale* or for strategic market objectives. An acquisition is an outright purchase of one company by an-

- other. Investment banks help facilitate the complexities that involve evaluations and financing for large complex transactions.

- A *leveraged buyout* is a fascinating type of acquisition in that a company's assets are used to help finance its own purchase. Leveraged buy-outs have helped to create an interesting breed of investor – the "corporate raider." This type of investor looks for undervalued and poorly managed companies with assets that can be leveraged (used as security for a loan) to finance a large portion of the purchase. The raider then improves the operations and profitability of the company and then "flips it" to another buyer for a large profit. Some call corporate raiders "vultures" but they provide a service in that they help purge out ineffective management who aren't realizing the true potential of a company and its assets. There is probably a good chance that the term "corporate raider" was created by the executives who were ousted from their jobs when the raider and his crew took over.

- Forming an *initial public offering* (IPO) requires specific expertise in working with the Security and Exchange Commission. An IPO is the process of taking a private company public. Going "public" means that anybody can buy shares of the company on a stock exchange. Hundreds of millions of dollars are created by convincing the investing public that a company is worthy of their owning some of its shares. The SEC makes sure that the public is protected from unscrupulous offerings and the investment bank helps the private company obtain approval and brings the new company to the public marketplace by marketing it to the retail securities industry and helping promote its initial offering on the stock exchange.

  When a company goes public, the owners of the private company usually become instant millionaires as the investing public buys paper shares for the exchange of cash with the hope of making money on the new company when the stock price increases in value. Meanwhile, the ex-owners of the company make millions on selling their ownership rights. The investment bank usually makes its money from commissions made from the sale of the IPO stock.

- *Offshore banks*, by definition, are located out of your home country and subject to the laws of where they are chartered. In many cases, offshore banks act as a marketplace where clients can have access to services not available in their home country. One of the most popular services that offshore banks can provide is bank secrecy and certain protections from home country civil laws and taxation regulations. Tax "havens" like in the Caribbean, Switzerland, the Channel Islands off England and other usually small countries have developed a major industry by becoming international banking centers.

5.3 HOW DO BANKS MAKE MONEY?

Banks are just like other businesses; however, their product is money. Other businesses sell products or services; banks sell money – in the form of loans, certificates of deposit

(CDs) and other financial products. Banks, just like other businesses, make money on the difference of what their products or services cost and at what cost they can sell the products or services to the end user – the bank customer.

For banks, the "raw product" is depositor funds, loans from other banks and income derived from lending and other service operations. Each product has its cost. In the case of depositor funds, interest is paid by the banks to depositors for the use of their funds when they purchase savings accounts, certificates of deposit, and money market accounts. When banks borrow from other banks or the Fed, the cost is interest on the loan. For each one of these cases, the interest rate charges are different; thus the cost of the raw product varies depending on the source.

Another large cost to the banks comes through normal operating expenses and capital investments. Banks have high administrative costs for personnel and banks are usually located in prime real estate locations. Moreover, new technology requires constant support and upgrading. All of these expenses need to be included in the cost of services sold by the banks.

As lending money is usually the largest profit center for a commercial bank, the "spread" is a key element. A spread is the difference between what interest and other fees a bank pays to borrow funds and what interest and other fees it can lend those funds for to customers. For instance, if a bank can borrow a loan from the Fed for 5.2% and lend those same funds for 8.2%, the bank has a spread of 3%. But operational expenses such as those discussed in the preceding paragraph must also be taken out of that spread.

Banks are not limited to just loaning money for its income revenue. A bank also generates revenue on countless numbers of administrative services, which are usually small but can add up to be significant. These administrative charges are a point for marketing the differences between banks who usually match very closely on most other costs.

Banks can also use borrowed money to invest in securities such as stocks and bonds. During the S&L crisis of the late 1980's, banks were using federally guaranteed loans to invest in risky investments and taxpayers eventually got stuck with the tab when the investments went south. Much tighter restrictions now exist on what types of equities a bank can invest in.

Bank-issued credit cards are part of a bank's strategic mix of products. Customers love credit cards and banks not only make profits from the high interest rates charged on outstanding balances but also charge the merchants transaction fees. Some banks offer secured credit cards with comparatively low interest rates but the majority of credit cards are unsecured. Given the risk factors associated with unsecured and impulsive purchasing, credit cards are a mixed blessing in that they justify very high interest rates but payment risk can put a big dent in the profitability if risks aren't controlled by using tools such as credit scoring.

Banks can be very successful, but they require excellent management due to the complexities, competition and thin profit margins. But keep in mind that banks are also key points of distribution of the money supply and if banks aren't doing well, the economy probably isn't far behind.

5.4 CORPORATE FORMATION AND STRUCTURE OF BANKS

You don't just rent some space, put out a sign and start taking deposits. Banks are much too important for that as they are an integral player in the financial system that supports our economy and way of life. Because of this fact, close scrutiny is given to the members of a banking company. The rules and requirements vary from state to state and depend on whether the bank wishes to become a member of the Federal Reserve System with all the benefits and responsibilities or seek being state chartered. As the people behind the banks are of major concern, the founding group of investors and operations personnel needs to be of the highest personal and professional character.

The Charter

A *charter* is a formal document that governs the manner in which the bank is regulated and operated. It authorizes the organization of the bank under either a state or federal agency. The agency that charters the bank is responsible for protecting the public from unsafe banking practices. The responsible agency not only does the investigation of the founding group of investors but also conducts regular on-site examinations to make sure the bank's financial condition is good and that the bank is complying with banking regulations. Many in the industry say that state and federal Bank charters typically do not differ too much in the way the bank conducts its daily operations but a federally chartered bank is usually considered safer in that it has direct access to the practically unlimited resources of the Federal Reserve discount window for low cost loans and the full backing of perhaps the most powerful institution in the economy.

Board of Directors

The organizing group has to identify directors, a chief executive officer (who usually must have past experience running a bank), and other executives. The integrity, past business, and credit histories of those people will greatly affect the acceptance or denial of the bank's application to obtain a charter. The important thing is to carefully select these partners and make sure they are team players, have the experience and know-how to help make the bank work, and can withstand the close scrutiny of the regulatory investigation.

Holding Company

A bank holding company is a *company* that has control over a bank. It holds at least 25 percent of the stock of the bank and has the ability to control the election of a majority of the directors of the bank. The Regulators may also determine that a company either directly or indirectly has controlling influence over certain management and policy decisions for the bank. The organizing group has the option of establishing a holding company for the bank when it applies for the charter but this in no way relieves close scrutiny or changes any of the rules.

Capital Requirements for Forming a Bank

The capital requirements to start a bank can vary greatly from state to state if it is seeking a state charter. For example, in Florida, the suggested capital requirement is $6 million for a bank in a metropolitan area and $4 million for a bank in a rural area. In other states, such as New York, that amount might be $10 million or more for metropolitan areas. Those capital requirements are usually determined by the strategic plan and pro forma financial statements for the local market.

Bank Services – Checking Account

The concept of checks has been around since about 352 B.C. in the Roman Empire. It appears that checks really started becoming popular in Holland in the 1500 to 1600s. Dutch "cashiers" – usually a goldsmith or jeweler – provided an alternative to keeping large amounts of cash at home and agreed to hold depositors' assets such as gold and jewelry for safekeeping. For a fee, they would pay the depositors' debts from the account based on a note that the depositors would write. Today's banks do the same thing. It became a little more complicated when lots of banks became involved and money needed to be shifted from one bank to the next. To make things easier, banks now have a system of check "*clearinghouses.*" Banks either send clear checks through the Federal Reserve or use a private clearinghouse to transfer the funds and clear the check. Here is a diagram of how it works.

Figure 4: How a check works:

5. The check is stamped as "paid" and your bank is credited with the amount which then gets credited to your account

4. The check is sent to the third party bank and debited to third party account

3. The check is sent to the nearest clearinghouse to the third party bank

1. You deposit a third party check into your account

2. The check is coded to your account and sent to the regional Fed bank

Banks offer lots of other financial products for their depositors. The checking account is just one of the most common. Checking is convenient because it lets you buy things without having to worry about carrying the cash – or using a credit card and paying its interest. While most checking accounts do not pay interest, some do – these are referred to as *negotiable order of withdrawal* (NOW) accounts.

Other Bank Services

Aside from checking accounts, banks offer loans (you pay the bank interest to borrow the money), Certificate of deposit (the bank pays you interest to borrow your money), money market accounts (the bank pays you interest), not to mention traditional savings accounts (the bank pays you interest to borrow your money). Most banks now also provide the capability for a customer to set up individual retirement accounts (IRAs) and other special retirement accounts like an educational savings account or medical savings accounts. Many larger banks also offer various forms of insurance and the ability to buy and sell stocks, bonds and mutual funds.

The following is a brief discussion of each:

- Savings accounts – This is probably the most familiar type of account, and these accounts usually require either a low minimum balance or have no minimum balance requirement, and allow you to keep your money in a safe place while it earns interest paid by the bank each month.

- Money market account – An account where monies deposited are invested in a secure mutual fund, which invests in secure low interest bearing instruments such as a U.S. government bonds fund or other low risk investments. Because the deposit monies are turned into shares, before a money market holder can get access to funds in the money market account, withdrawals from a money market are usually restricted to a limited number of withdrawals within a certain period. MMAs usually provide a way to earn interest and have limited access to deposits.

- Certificates of deposit: This type of account provides higher than money market interest but without the flexibility of access to the deposited amounts.

- Individual retirement accounts and education savings accounts: These types of accounts require that you have a trustee to make sure that monies deposited are in compliance with regulations that allow for investments to grow without paying taxes. An IRA is a vehicle for long term savings and investment with the objective of promoting funding for retirement. There can be penalties with these types of accounts if the money is used for something other than retirement or education.

- Stocks, bonds and mutual funds: Many larger regional banks also offer brokerage services for securities investors. In 1999 the Glass-Steagal Act, which had formerly separated the equity investments from banking, was repealed and banks either purchased existing brokerage agencies or started their own. This ability also allows them to service the various types of IRA accounts.

- Insurance: The amendment of Glass-Steagal also removed the separation between banks and the insurance industry. Banks have now become a "one-stop shopping" destination for most financial transactions needed by individuals and businesses.

Financing a Home and a Car Through a Bank

One of the most fundamental services that banks offer is loans for homes and autos. Owning either or both is a rite of passage for most Americans and a dream for most citizens of less developed nations. The following is a description of the basic procedures for obtaining a mortgage (home loan) or an auto loan.

5.5 OBTAINING A MORTGAGE AND AN AUTO LOAN

Once you've decided to buy a home, it's recommended that you go to several banks to find out how much a bank will lend you. Most banks follow the same procedures. The variation is in types of mortgages, interest rates, closing costs and loan terms.

Things you will need to provide the bank for a mortgage qualification:
- Proof of income for the past several years
- Credit statement
- Personal financial statement
- Proof of savings or other means of paying for the down payment.

You will sit down with a bank loan officer and they will qualify what types of loans are available and what the interest rates and terms are for each. Once you and the bank loan officer have decided on which loan might be best for you, the personal information you provide will undergo a process of verification. Accordingly, your income, net worth (your assets less all your debts) and credit history will be analyzed. As a rule of thumb, banks will lend up to twice yearly gross income; however, the actual process is much more complex; the loan department has a checklist of requirements you must meet in order to determine exactly what risks a loan to you might pose. Once they establish what category of loan they can lend you, you can get a provisional letter of qualification. This will give you an excellent idea of what price ranges you can realistically afford. Unfortunately, most people don't find out how much they can qualify for before shopping for a home and wait until they have made an emotional commitment to a particular property. That's when many home buyers get into a position of overextension and obtain financing which may exceed their capability to support. (There are many ways to finance a home but that's not within the scope of this book.)

Once you find a home and negotiate a price, you sign a contract with the seller. You take the contract to the bank and the bank now requires due diligence on the property; after all, they will be the "owner of last recourse" for the property. They will ask that the property be appraised by a licensed real estate appraiser, a title search made to be sure that the sellers actually own the property and to ascertain what loans or liens are secured by the property as these must be paid off before the bank will accept the loan. Also, the bank will recommend that the buyer have a home inspection to make sure there is no leaky roof and all other systems (A/C, plumbing, electrical and appliances) are in good condition.

During this period, the buyer usually ties up the property (takes it off the market) by placing a deposit on the property into an *escrow account*. This account is placed with the bank or a third party acting as a neutral entity until all monetary and legal requirements of the purchase contract are fulfilled.

Once the property has been appraised, the bank will usually lend a certain percentage of the sale price or the appraised value, whichever is most conservative. Typically, if a buyer wants to put the minimum down payment, the bank may finance up to 95% of the price depending on the buyer's financial and credit profile. The bank will place the loan amount in the escrow account and from this loan amount will be deducted any monies for outstanding loans or liens against the property. Other closing costs such as a title search and insurance, and other loan charges will also be deducted from the loan amount or paid out of pocket by either buyer or seller depending on the terms of the purchase contract. Once all expenses associated with the transaction are deducted from the escrow account, whatever is leftover is paid out to the seller and the title of the property and the loan agreement are given to the buyer.

Obtaining an Auto Loan

An auto loan is similar to a home loan in that the bank is the ultimate buyer of recourse and all title and appraisal requirements must be met before the car is yours. Once you find a car you want to purchase, you negotiate a price and the dealer will give you details on the car that will allow the bank to access the data on the type, make and model and tell you how much they will loan on the car. Usually, a bank will finance 90% of a new car. If you finance the car, you will be required to have full insurance coverage to protect the bank's interest. Once the bank agrees to lend you the money on the auto, they transfer or issue a check to the dealer and you are issued a temporary license and registration for the car and away you go. That's all there is to it. Auto loans are high profit transactions for the bank and the bank's due diligence is much less stringent than when you are obtaining a mortgage.

5.6 BANK OPERATIONS

Bank operations are regulated by Federal and State Banking authorities and the Credit Union Administration, depending on the particular bank charter. However, from an operational aspect, much depends on what additional services a bank offers. For example, a bank that offers a securities brokerage would also need to meet regulation and compliance with the Security and Exchange Commission (SEC). If the bank also offers insurance products, the state insurance commission would be the regulator.

The following is a general overview of banking operations, which also determine in large part the management structure for a typical bank.

1. Compliance: As banks are under scrutiny from regulators, a department is dedicated to making sure the bank operates within guidelines and is in total compliance with rules and regulations. Many operational functions need to pass through compliance before the bank is approved.

2. Deposit function: As deposits are the fundamental element in a bank's success and ability to function as an ongoing business, careful attention is given to tracking net deposits as this determines the leverage available for lending and the generation of income from loans.

3. Checking and negotiable items: Although most checking activities are free to many patrons, it is still an important service for customer retention and other financial opportunities. As a bank is a distribution point for most forms of money, a bank must be knowledgeable about all forms of negotiable instruments like: bank checks, letters of credit, wire transfers, and others. Most banks may charge for these services and they are part of the bank's revenue stream.

4. Payments and collections: Almost all lending activities require regular, periodic payments – some from customers (loans) and some to customers (interest on savings, CDs, money markets). Payments create not only profits from the interest but also create the necessary operational cash flow. Making sure that loans are being paid is a vital part of operations. Also, banks facilitate payments to and from customers – particularly through online banking, which has helped to not only add value for the customer but also reduce the labor cost of providing some services.

5. Fraud and loss control: As technology plays a more important role in all banking activities, fraud, money laundering and computer hackers have made this role an important function. Bank fraud in the U.S. alone is estimated to cost billions of dollars each year!

6. Lending functions: This is the heart of the banking business. Banks make money on the spread between what they pay for money and what they can lend it for. Banks find capital for lending by taking out loans from the Federal Reserve

banking systems by leveraging (using the fractional reserve as a deposit), borrowing from other banks, or issuing stocks and bonds directly on the exchanges.

Making profitable loans is a matter of qualifying risks. The procedure is highly regimented but there are always unforeseen risks in the future and the loan department attempts to limit non-performing loans as a priority function. When evaluating an application for loans, the higher the risks, the higher the spread. Because of industry competition, banks operate on very narrow profit margins and containing non-performing loans is serious business.

7. Fund management and bank investments: Banks are always looking for ways to make a profitable spread and it is not just limited to loans. Banks will also invest in other liquid investments such as stocks and bonds. Part of sound investing is to have a diversified portfolio of investments. Although banks have most of their funds in mortgages and other banking instruments, a portion of funds are in other types of vehicles to help provide diversification and – in some cases – higher profit margins. Most banks have a Trust department which may act as investment advisors for customers and require bank specialists solely dedicated to that function.

8. Internal audit: In conjunction with Fraud and Loss control and Compliance departments, banks do regular audits not only to monitor for transaction anomalies but also to measure overall bank performance. All larger enterprises have this function but not to the extent and importance as found in the banking industry.

9. Marketing and customer service: Banking is mainly a commodity service and companies need to work hard to differentiate themselves from the competition. Moreover, banks understand that building a relationship with customers requires consistent and excellent customer service. After all, money is near and dear to most of us. Banking is a relationship business and most banks excel at providing excellent service. Moreover, it costs about nine times as much to obtain a new customer as it does to maintain an existing customer.

10. Digital banking: More and more customers are going online to do their financial transactions. As a result, the information technology and support is fast becoming a critical part of operations and customer service departments. Banks have hitched themselves to technology and infrastructure costs are one of the major motivators for bank mergers as transaction costs decline with the numbers of transactions.

11. Additional services: Many banks now offer insurance, stock, bond and mutual funds and require a separate operation and specialized personnel. As a result of new and complex operations falling under different regulatory bodies and regulations, many banks have changed corporate structure to become holding companies with different specialized companies under one umbrella.

 6.0 Non-Bank Finance

6.1 PUBLIC MARKET FINANCING

The largest pool of non-bank funding can be found in the world's 337 different stock and bond and commodity markets (33 in the U.S. alone). Companies who want to expand without incurring large interest charges can choose to sell shares to the public. This is called *equity financing*. Governments may need to raise funds in addition to tax revenue and offer interest bearing bonds to the public. Companies also offer interest bearing bonds to the public as an alternative to equity financing or as an alternative to bank financing.

6.2 PRIVATE INVESTMENT COMPANIES AND SYNDICATES

Private investment groups are when usually high wealth individuals form an association and pool investment funds. They invest in any project that meets the group's investment objectives and often these groups are made up of local investors who invest in real estate ventures as part of an overall strategy of investment diversification.

6.3 VENTURE CAPITALISTS

Venture capitalists normally play a part in the evolutionary step between an entity being simply a small company, and going public. These companies will lend private money to help small promising companies grow to a point where they can go public. Venture capitalists usually lend money with interest and/or take a pre-public offering ownership position and hope to cash in when the company goes public.

6.4 LEASING COMPANIES

Oftentimes, corporations that sell specialized industrial equipment will team up with a company or form a subsidiary company to finance capital equipment lease-purchases. The reason they do this is that the equipment is specialized and if there is a default on the lease or loan payments, the leaser can take possession of the equipment and place it with other clients or resell to other clients. Banks usually don't have this kind of recourse on specialty equipment and leave this niche to the specialists' leasing companies. Moreover, leasing companies are a powerful tool in marketing and sales of expensive special-use equipment.

6.5 PRIVATE OR SECOND MORTGAGES

Home owners who have no mortgage on their homes may offer to finance the sale of their home. They usually don't need the cash and prefer to make a higher interest rate by financing the sale of their home. It can be a win-win for both seller and buyer as the buyer may get a very competitive rate and the seller can make a higher return than with other conservative investments; moreover, the seller can use the title of the home as security for the loan.

More common is the practice of obtaining private financing to cover any shortfall in the cash down payment on a property purchase. Here's how it works:

Suppose you make an offer on a home that costs $250,000. You go to the bank and determine that they will lend you 85% of the purchase price ($212,500). That means you have to come up with the difference ($37,500). There is a problem in that you only have $27,500. You really want the home so you have several choices. First, and most common, you turn to your family to borrow $10,000 for the balance of the down payment. Second, you can ask the seller to "carry a second mortgage" for the $10,000. The seller will require interest and a legal document to secure a second legal ownership position behind that of the bank who will lend the money for the first mortgage ($212,500). Third, you can seek bank or private mortgage company financing for the $10,000, which will usually cost more interest than obtaining a loan from family or the seller (normally, the seller wants the deal to go through and will make the loan for a short period).

6.6 SUB-PRIME MORTGAGE LENDING

Contrary to what you might think, the term sub-prime does not refer to a favorable interest rate below that of the Prime rate paid to the most qualified borrowers but to borrowers with weak credit. (Do marketing people know how to spin a name?) Non-bank financing attracts those individuals or companies who would not qualify under national bank lending standards, such as borrowers with high leverage, negative net worth, recent losses, and those faced with fast growth/expansion needs.

Normally, sub-prime mortgages are funded by non-bank financing mortgage lenders. Bad credit history for sub-prime borrowers who have stable incomes may not meet the debt service ratios of the traditional lending institutions and the borrowers have no recourse but to turn to sub-prime lenders. Alternative or Sub-prime lenders who are providing such mortgages normally charge interest rates 1.5% to 3% higher than traditional prime borrower's rates from the banks and usually require more down payment and higher loan fees.

Recently, there has been a problem with sub-prime lenders as mortgage defaults in this category have increased. The sudden panic caused by this news is not so much the potential failure of a few lending companies but the effect that a glut of houses for sale on the market might have on home values and the effect it might have on equity devaluation that other banks and institutions have in non sub-prime real estate.

6.7 ASSET-BASED LENDING

Companies with cash flow problems or immediate financing needs may turn to a specialized financing called asset-base lending. Most companies allow customers to pay within 30 days. For many reasons, customers will take possession of goods or services and not be able to comply with the normal payment terms. When this happens, the holder of the accounts receivable may become short on cash to finance ongoing operations. If all other forms of traditional financing are no longer available, companies may be forced to turn to asset-based lenders. Typically, a company can secure a high interest loan based on a percentage of the accounts receivables. The account receivables go to the lending company to pay back the loan and interest.

Another way to obtain short-term cash flow financing is to lend on the equity value of machinery and inventory. These are also high interest loans and usually used only when there is no other recourse.

7.0 Central Banking

The functions of central banks have been talked about previously, but this institution plays such an important part in today's modern economy that the subject requires a more in-depth discussion. Although there are slight variations between countries and regions, the model of the U.S. Federal Reserve Banking system serves as a benchmark.

Today, the U.S. Federal Reserve Systems duties fall into four general areas:

- Conducting the nation's monetary policy by influencing the monetary and credit conditions in the economy in pursuit of maximum employment, stable prices, and moderate long-term interest rates

- Supervising and regulating banking institutions to ensure the safety and soundness of the nation's banking and financial system and to protect the credit rights of consumers

- Maintaining the stability of the financial system and containing systemic risk that may arise in financial markets

- Providing financial services to depository institutions, the U.S. government, and foreign official institutions, including playing a major role in operating the nation's payments system

7.1 BRIEF HISTORY OF THE U.S. FEDERAL RESERVE BANK

At the end of the nineteenth and twentieth centuries, there had been numerous financial panics that plagued the nation. The numerous private banks were just like other business ventures and some thrived and others went bust. But banks seemed to have a much more dire impact on local economies when they were forced to close their doors. The failure of the nation's loosely organized banking system to effectively provide consistent funding to the rapidly growing economy had made for a series of local financial panics.

Authorities and economists of the time saw that the availability of short-term credit was an important source of liquidity when a bank experienced unexpected and widespread withdrawals during a financial panic. A particularly severe crisis in 1907 prompted Congress to establish the *National Monetary Commission*, which proposed that the government create an institution that would help prevent and contain financial disruptions. After years of considerable debate, Congress passed the Federal Reserve Act "to provide for the establishment of Federal Reserve banks, to furnish an elastic money supply, to afford means of rediscounting commercial paper, to establish a more effective supervision of banking in the United States, and for other purposes." President Woodrow Wilson finally signed the act into law on December 23, 1913.

After the creation of the Federal Reserve, it became clear that the act had much broader implications for national economic and financial policy. A series of acts and amendments were added to address the issues that grew from the steady increase in the power and influence that the Fed was accumulating in the course of its evolution. Moreover, Congress enacted further clarification of how the Fed should be further tasked with economic responsibilities to define the Fed's role in guiding the economy toward full employment, control of inflation and exchange rates.

Recent history saw the Fed's growing stature take center stage when the oil crisis of the 1970's and 80's created double digit inflation and the worst U.S economy since the Great Depression of the 1930s. Someone needed to put the genie back in the bottle and enforce the economic medicine needed to get the economy back on track. In 1979, Paul Volcker, the former President of the Federal Reserve Bank of New York, was appointed by President Jimmy Carter to become the Chairman of the Board of Governors of the U.S. Federal Reserve System and he stepped up to the challenge. Volcker had to withstand considerable political pressure and enforce the discipline necessary to achieve eventual stability.

Volcker made a fundamental change in how the Fed approached the economy and abandoned the previous policy of targeting interest rates and started focusing on the growth of money supply. In 1981, inflation peaked at 13.5 % while most retail commercial loan interest rates were above 18%. The U.S. economy was in a stage of *"stagflation"* (where the economy is stagnant with high inflation), but by implementing tight monetary policies and forcing a recession by 1983, inflation was lowered to 3.2% and set the stage for over 20 years of sustained economic growth and low inflation. After tromping inflation and helping set the stage for the good times to come, Mr. Volcker stepped down in 1987 and was replaced by Alan Greenspan who took the baton and continued to place the Fed in the economic limelight. In 2006, Mr. Greenspan retired and was replaced by the current Board chairman, Ben Bernanke.

7.2 STRUCTURE OF THE FEDERAL RESERVE SYSTEM

Congress designed the structure of the Federal Reserve System to give it a broad perspective on the economy and on economic activity in all parts of the nation. It is a federal system in that the oversight of the Fed is the responsibility of Congress, but the actual ownership structure is much more complex and controversial. The Fed is composed of twelve regional Federal Reserve Banks, the Board of Governors in Washington, D.C., and the Federal Open Market Committee (FOMC).

The Board and the Reserve Banks share responsibility for supervising and regulating certain financial institutions and activities, for providing banking services to depository institutions and the federal government, and for ensuring that consumers receive adequate information and fair treatment in their business with the banking system.

Board of Governors

The Board is composed of seven members, who are appointed by the President of the United States and confirmed by the U.S. Senate. The full term of a Board member is fourteen years, and the appointments are staggered so that one term expires on January 31 of each even-numbered year. After serving a full term, a Board member may not be reappointed. However, there are some exceptions to the rule. The Chairman and the Vice Chairman of the Board are also appointed by the President and confirmed by the Senate. The nominees to these posts must already be members of the Board or must be simultaneously appointed to the Board. The terms for these positions are four years.

The Board of Governors is supported by a staff in Washington, D.C., numbering about 1,800 as of 2004.

The Board's responsibilities require thorough analysis of domestic and international financial and economic developments. The Board carries out those responsibilities in conjunction with other components of the Federal Reserve System. Even though the

FOMC (Federal Open Market Committee) establishes open market operations, the Board of Governors has sole authority over changes in reserve requirements, and it must approve any change in the discount rate initiated by a Federal Reserve Bank.

The Board also plays a major role in the supervision and regulation of the U.S. banking system. It has supervisory responsibilities for state-chartered banks that are members of the Federal Reserve System, bank holding companies (companies that control banks), the foreign activities of member banks, the U.S. activities of foreign banks, and Edge Act and agreement corporations (limited-purpose institutions that engage in a foreign banking business). The Board also supervises approximately 900 state member banks and 5,000 bank holding companies.

Other federal agencies as delegated by the Federal Reserve also serve as primary federal supervisors of commercial banks. For example, the *Office of the Comptroller of the Currency* supervises national banks, and the *Federal Deposit Insurance Corporation* supervises state banks that are not members of the Federal Reserve System.

Members of the Board of Governors are constantly called before Congress and frequently testify before congressional committees on the economy, monetary policy, banking supervision and regulation, consumer credit protection, financial markets, and other matters.

For instance, the Chairman of the Board of Governors testifies before the Senate Committee on Banking, Housing, and Urban Affairs and the House Committee on Financial Services on or about February 20 and July 20 of each year as required by the Federal Reserve Act. This presentation is called the "Humphrey-Hawkins Testimony."

7.3 ROLE OF THE FOMC AND HOW FED FUNDS RATES ARE ESTABLISHED

The Federal Open Market Committee (FOMC) is made up of the members of the Board of Governors, the president of the Federal Reserve Bank of New York, and the presidents of four other Federal Reserve Banks. *The FOMC oversees open market operations, which is the main tool used by the Federal Reserve to influence overall monetary and credit conditions.* More specifically, the Federal Reserve implements monetary policy through its control over the federal funds rate—the rate at which depository institutions borrow funds from each other. The FOMC exercises this control by influencing the demand for and supply of money through the following means:

- Open market operations—the purchase or sale of securities, primarily U.S. Treasury securities, in the open market to influence the level of balances that depository institutions hold at the Federal Reserve Banks

- Reserve requirements—requirements regarding the percentage of certain deposits that depository institutions must hold in reserve in the form of cash or in an account at a Federal Reserve Bank
- Contractual clearing balances—an amount that a depository institution agrees to hold at its Federal Reserve Bank in addition to any required reserve balance
- Discount window lending—extensions of credit to depository institutions made through the primary, secondary, or seasonal lending programs

For example, banks routinely borrow cash reserves from other banks or lend reserves to other banks to help provide liquidity in the banking system. An active market exists for interbank loans of reserves. This market is called the *federal funds market*, because the reserves that are traded are immediately available to satisfy Federal Reserve requirements. The interest rate charged on such loans is called the *federal funds rate*.

By increasing or decreasing the quantity of reserves in the banking system, the Fed can lower or raise the federal funds rate. Suppose the Fed determines that it should raise its federal funds rate target to 6%, from its current level of 5.5%. *Then the Fed sells bonds on the open market, reducing the supply of reserves in the banking system and pushing the federal funds rate upward.*

Figure 5: Adjusting money supply to affect the Fed Funds rate

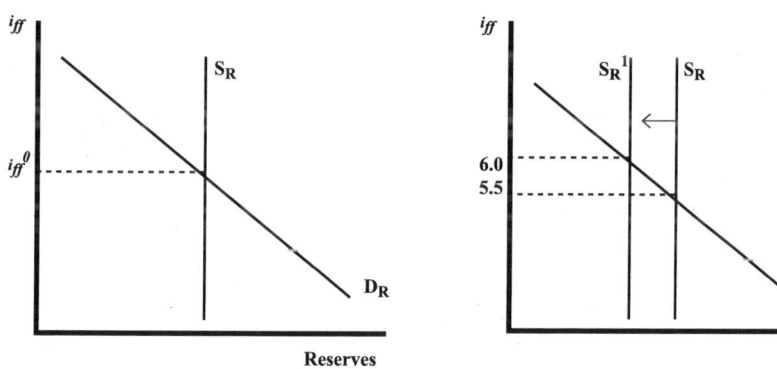

S_R = Money supply before Fed action; S_R^1 = Money supply after Fed sells reserves in the form of government bonds to the open market and reduces the money supply of loanable reserves.

D_R = demand that remains constant, and as a result of shifting money supply at Sr^1 the interest rate will move up from 5.5 % to 6%.

7.4 HOW THE FED FUNDS RATE AFFECTS RETAIL LOAN RATES

By decreasing the amount of money for loans, banks are forced to raise the rates charged to customers. The demand for loanable bank funds is determined by the desire of businesses and individuals to finance investment projects and purchases. Obviously, firms and individuals are willing to borrow more when the interest rate is seen as being feasible for making a profit. As the cost of borrowing gets more expensive, projects and investments start losing return as a result of increasing loan costs. As a result, the demand for loans will decrease. Eventually, less demand for money will have a cooling effect on the economy.

Figure 6: Effect of interest rates on loan demand

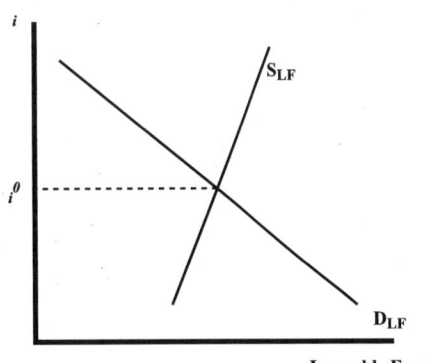

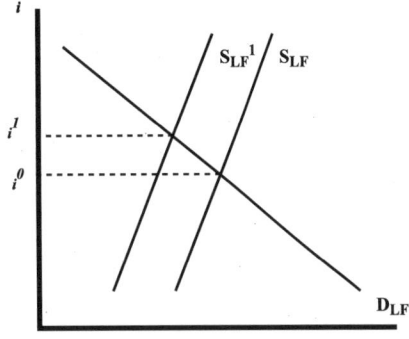

A sale of bonds by the Federal Reserve, which decreases the supply of reserves and increases the federal funds rate, causes banks to raise their interest rate and offer fewer loans. The supply of loanable funds shifts to the left, and the market interest rate rises.

7.5 HOW THE FED FUNDS RATE AFFECTS AGGREGATE DEMAND FOR GOODS AND SERVICES

When the Fed pushes the interest rates upward, it typically also increases the expected *real interest rate* (interest rate less inflation rate). The increase in the expected real interest rate reduces the demand for investment by businesses. But a reduction in investment spending by businesses also reduces aggregate demand because workers become pessimistic or uncertain about the future and put off some purchases that might have otherwise been made. The reduction in demand as a result of higher interest rates can become a self-fulfilling prophecy in that an *anticipated* reduction in demand for goods and services means that there will eventually be less demand for workers. Eventually, the positive result of lowering demand will be a reduction of pressure on prices.

Because demand needs to work its way down the production chain, it takes time for the Fed funds rate changes to have an impact on the economy. As a result, the Fed needs to anticipate inflation and move quickly to keep it from becoming a detriment to the economy.

When the Fed wants to *stimulate t*he economy, The Fed reverses the process and creates reserves by *purchasing U.S. Treasury securities* on the open market. When the Fed buys bonds, it injects reserves into the banking system. When there is a greater supply of funds, interest rates decrease to promote the movement of excess funds. As a result, banks can loan to customers at a lower rate and still keep the profit spread. The increase in loans and investments will eventually create increased demand for goods and services and businesses will have need for more employees, which begets more consumers and increases demand even further. Then the Fed starts to worry again.

The balancing of money supply, interest rates, inflation and aggregate demand is the delicate balance that the Fed is charged with. Recently, the growth of globalization has had a positive impact on prices and interest rates as new low cost producers (China, Mexico, India, etc.) help keep downward pressure on price increases and thus help to keep interest rates down. On the other side of the coin, as new economies start to flourish there will be pressures on prices as more new consumers suck up the supply of goods and services. Today, increased demand for commodities to fuel the growth in emerging markets such as China and India has been pushing up prices on basic materials and putting upward pressure on the PPI (producer price index). Eventually this may put pressure on global prices and the Fed and other central banks will need to take action to curb the threat of inflation. The trick – as always – will be to stifle inflationary expectations without stifling local and global economies.

7.6 CONSTANT VIGILANCE

Since it takes time to wring inflation from the system, the Fed takes great pains to avoid letting inflation become established in the economy. As a result, the Fed constantly monitors a host of economic variables in an attempt to determine where the economy is relative to a benchmark output level. The variables the Fed pays most attention to include the following:

- How rapidly aggregate demand is growing compared to the estimated sustainable growth rate (about 4%-4.5% GDP growth rate)
- The unemployment rate and the behavior of employment costs
- Commodity prices
- The extent of manufacturing inventories and backorders (orders that can't be filled immediately)
- Global economic conditions

These indicators provide Federal Reserve policymakers and economists with important information on the probable behavior of prices. The Fed estimates the growth of aggregate demand by estimating growth in the labor force and how rapidly the capital stock (machinery and other means of production) is growing, and if productivity is improving.

The unemployment rate is an indicator of the demand for labor, which is an indirect indicator of what myriad businesses see as the need to increase production. When the unemployment rate is low, it can also demonstrate that production is near maximum levels and that demand may soon push up prices. Moreover, if labor leaders see that there is scarcity of available labor, workers have a lever to demand higher wages. Higher wages will normally be passed on to consumers. Low unemployment usually is followed by increasing prices – but not always. High unemployment is an indicator of a weak economy with low demand for goods and services. Usually, high unemployment is an end result of high inflation after interest rates have been increased to bring down the rate of inflation via decreasing demand for money.

As commodities are usually basic to the production process, if commodity prices increase, there will be price increases at the retail level. Thus, the Fed may "tighten" monetary policy when they observe commodity prices rising (as seems to be happening today).

Inventories and backorders are a measure of demand and the ability of the manufacturing sector to meet product demand. When inventories are high, firms are not likely to raise prices because they may have excess goods and need to reduce the product inventory. However, when inventories are low and backorders are high, that usually means demand at the retail level is high and backorders may indicate that demand may outstrip the capability of manufacturers to meet the demand. This situation gives firms more market power, and price increases are more likely.

Globalization and global economic conditions can affect the local economy in important ways. For example, should Europe move into a strong economic expansion, Fed policymakers would most likely expect the demand for U.S. exports to increase to help fill some of the European demand. An increase in net exports would cause aggregate demand to increase, putting more pressure on prices. The Fed might act to reduce domestic spending (through higher interest rates) to offset the increase in net exports. Moreover, higher interest rates in the U.S. might increase the exchange rate of the dollar and make U.S. goods more expensive in foreign markets.

Juggling with Sharp Knives

Because economic adjustments by the Fed can have unexpected effects, changes need to be made with great deliberation and expertise. In reality, many of the factors the Fed pays particular attention to are not always predictive and as the global economy expands, collecting transparent data from other economies can make the interconnect between domestic and international monetary policy a difficult task. Because the Fed needs to be careful of what it says, a whole industry has been developed in an attempt to fathom the depths of Fed opinion; however, even experienced Fed watchers are never completely sure of what Fed policymakers will do in any particular instance. Yet, if you understand the basic elements of the interplay of how money supply affects interest rates and how interest rates can affect the economy, you will have come a long way toward understanding how the Federal Reserve influences monetary policy.

7.7 THE U.S. DOLLAR AND THE LENDER OF LAST RESORT (LOLR)

In 2000, one well-known U.S. Federal Reserve System market observer, Allen Sinai, made the comment:

> "The Greenspan Federal Reserve appears to have shifted regime, operating with a new policy framework that takes the world economy and financial system into account, viewing the U.S. as one component in this system."

Since the Bretton Woods agreement in 1944, which established a postwar international monetary system of convertible currencies, fixed exchange rates and free trade, the U.S. dollar has been the international currency of choice. This suggests that an additional burden was placed on the U.S. treasury and Federal Reserve System to provide not only a proper domestic money supply, but also a large international supply of U.S. dollars as well. Excess money supply can be the bane of inflation control. As a result, the U.S.

fed has to keep a close eye on the international money supply as well. Also, this suggests that the Federal Reserve – as the supplier of the dominant international reserve asset – should recognize that when it tightens domestic policy (thereby restricting the supply of international reserves), policy moves can be magnified or made more potent. In fact, it has been shown that many foreign central banking systems are highly sensitive to what the U.S. Fed does. Since the U.S. Federal Reserve is the ultimate supplier of international reserve assets, maintaining liquidity makes the U.S. Fed the "Lender of Last Resort" (LOLR) with all the attendant responsibilities.

In short, evidence indicates that changes in U.S. monetary policy have had a potent impact on the interest rates in emerging market economies. No doubt that wide-spread dollarization suggests that changes in U.S. monetary policy may have an important impact on the many users of U.S. dollars.

Most member countries of the EU have adopted the Euro as the common currency and this helps to provide some international currency asset diversification but it will be a long time before the Euro will supplant the supply of U.S. dollars. Just trying to match the quantity of U.S. dollars in the world economy would cause Euro inflation as the supply of Euros would far exceed the demand for them.

7.8 FED CONTROVERSY

Skeptics have been raising questions about the Federal Reserve System and suggest that it is a sham and – in fact – an entity controlled by the world's elite bankers and industrialist families. For one thing, it is true that the U.S. Fed is really not owned by the Federal government as the name implies. The Fed is owned by member banks that in turn are owned by stockholders. Just who these stockholders are has been the object of much investigation. Also, the independence of the Fed from political meddling is not completely genuine in that the President appoints the Board and Chairman. However, innuendos aside, there can be little doubt that a large and complex economic system needs structure, coordination and standardization as well as some clear accountability.

Some believe that credit is a dangerous thing. Many believe that the ability to control money supply with relative impunity is a ticking time bomb or a tool for total domination. But over the past twenty or thirty years, tremendous world wide economic growth, progress and prosperity has been fomented largely by credit and controlled rather nicely by the world's financial components led by the central banks. The new "emerging markets" (i.e. China, India, Brazil, Russia, Indonesia, Mexico) have demonstrated that the western model of money and banking is capable of great economic progress as opposed to centrally controlled economies.

The future of money and banking may very well be the mechanism that unites the world's economies through technology, uniform policies and procedures, to allow instantaneous and low cost transactions, which will support a vibrant world economy. But as someone once said "Whoever controls the money supply, controls the power" and citizens and the representatives in government need to ensure that transparency and accountability make those in the non-elected positions of real power (controlling the money supply) realize the trust and responsibility they have been given.

 8.0 International Finance

There are several definitions of International Finance. One is that International Finance is the branch of economics that studies the dynamics of exchange rates, international trade and foreign investment. Another simplifies things by stating that International Finance involves any financial transaction that happens between different countries. A third definition defines it as the study of international financial transactions, transactions that have some cross-border element with respect to payment, credit or investment, or a financial contract (Dufey and Chung 1990). Whatever definition, the growing intertwining of the world's economies makes the line that distinguishes foreign from domestic more and more difficult to define. For example, when a country purposefully tries to devalue its currency to make its exports more competitive (by decreasing interest rates and increasing the money supply), domestic inflation may be a consequence. Suffice it to say, international finance has its practical and theoretical sides, but for the purposes of this e-book, we will confine our discussion to the basics.

8.1 INTERNATIONAL TRADE, COMPARATIVE ADVANTAGE AND EXCHANGE RATES

International finance evolved to facilitate international trade. From the earliest times of primitive trading tribes, *comparative advantage* played a major role. If one tribe was good at producing bronze spearheads and a neighboring tribe produced high quality pottery, both groups would benefit from trade with each other. The two main questions were (and are today): How to value a good from a foreign tribe (or country) and how to pay for the good in such a way that would be acceptable to the foreign producer?

In the 19th century, David Ricardo, a British political economist, developed the theory of *comparative advantage*. The theory states simply that even if a country could produce everything more efficiently than another country, it would reap gains from specializing in what it was best at producing and trading with other nations for items it could produce but not as efficiently. For example, Peru is rich in copper. It could invest in developing other industries, but more profit could be gained by focusing on its natural advantage of having large and high quality copper reserves. The United States, on the other hand, is better served by investing in its capacity to produce technology and importing most of its copper from Peru. Both countries benefit by focusing on what they do best (with greater profit margins for each).

But how does the United States pay for the Peruvian copper? Peruvians use the Peruvian Nuevo sol as their domestic currency. U.S. dollars with pictures of dead gringos on them mean little to Peruvians trying to purchase an Inca Cola at a local bodega. By the same token, the Peruvian sol has no value in the U.S. So, there needs to be a means of exchanging values with practical results for both parties. Thus, the need for creating a way to reconvert foreign currency into local currency.

8.2 CURRENCY EXCHANGE RATES

In today's world, exchange rates are of two types: Floating and Pegged currencies.

Floating currencies: Major trading nations whose domestic economies have a high degree of transparency usually let the marketplace – or Foreign Exchange Market (known as the FOREX) – decide what a nation's currency is worth by a system of "bid and ask pricing." Here's an example of how it works.

In Germany, the local currency is the Euro (since 2002). When a German company sells an order to a U.S. importer, it makes its price quotation in Euros. Let's say the importer places an order for a German product with a total price of €100,000 (Euros). The importer, however, has no Euros in its bank account. How will it pay for the order in Euros? The importer will turn to its bank to purchase Euros to pay for the order. When the order is accepted by the importer, the bank will take dollars out of the importer's account and buy Euros at the "spot price" (price being quoted at the time of the Euro purchase) to send to the exporter's bank in Germany. On the day the importer formally accepts the order from Germany, the bank orders its foreign exchange traders to purchase the U.S. dollar equivalent of €100,000. The bank trader accesses the FOREX and buys €100,000 at an exchange rate of the latest FOREX quote of $1.3631 for each Euro for a total of $136,310 for the €100,000. The €100,000 in Euros is then sent to be credited to the account of the exporter in Germany and the importer's account is debited for the $136,310 plus any bank charges for the transaction.

Money & Banking

 U.S. Importer places order with German firm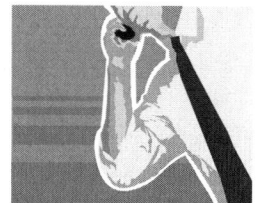

 German Exporter sends order and it is accepted by Importer

 Importer tells his bank to pay exporter the contract price in Euros

 U.S Bank purchases Euros on the FOREX

 Importer's bank sends the Euro payment to an international clearing agency to be sent to Exporter

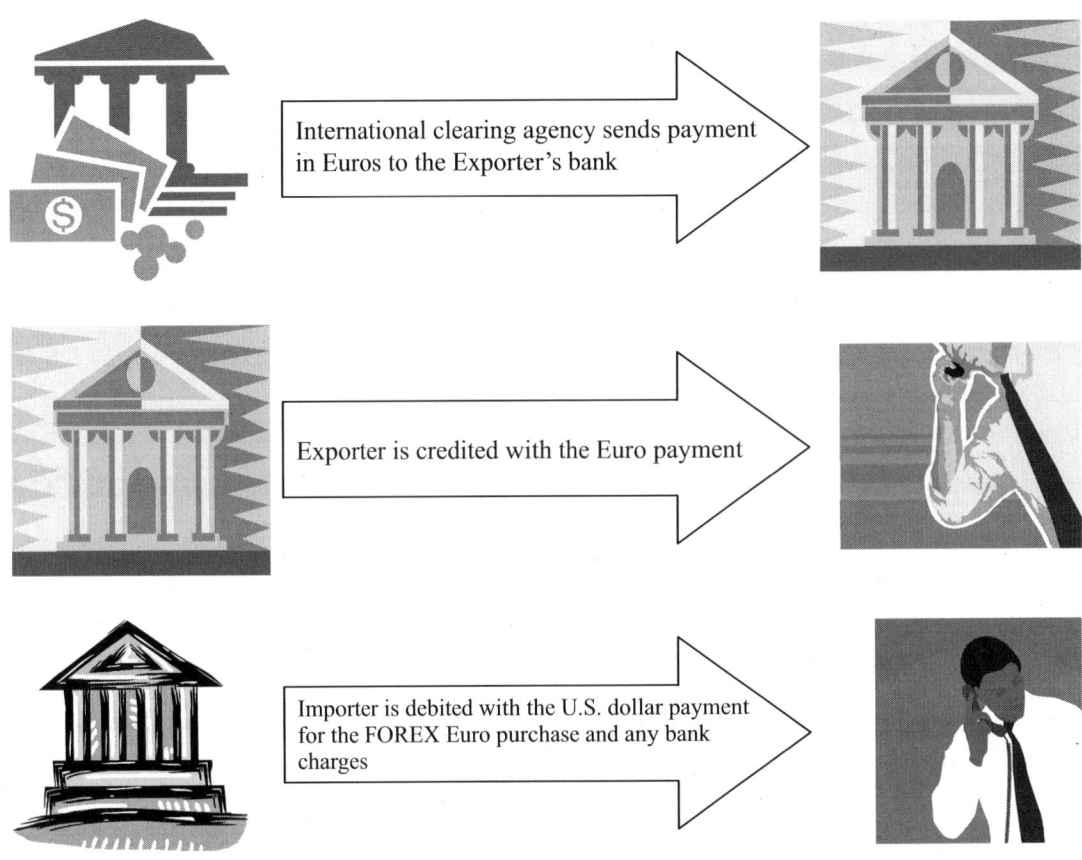

Factors Affecting Floating Currencies

Supply and demand: As with other commodities, if there is a large demand for a currency, there will be upward pressure on the *relative cost* of the currency. Conversely, if there is less demand for the available supply of a currency, the currency will stay relatively stable or depreciate against other currencies that are in demand.

Domestic factors: If the currency market (made up of banks, governments and speculators) perceives domestic, political or economic factors that may effect the future value of the particular nation's currency, the market will react accordingly. For example, if there is uncertainty within a country, trading partners may be concerned that the local production and financial infrastructure might become affected. As a result, importers who normally buy from the troubled nation will look elsewhere for other trading partners and the demand for the troubled exporting nation's currency will decrease (become weaker) and imports to the troubled nation will become more expensive. All of these potential results from perceived problems (they might not be real) can have an almost instant impact on the value of a nation's currency.

Other domestic factors that have a major impact on exchange rates are: domestic inflation, interest rates, national debt, GDP, and many of the same factors that affect the domestic economy. Many economists and lending institutions view a currency's exchange rate as an important indicator of how well a nation is doing in an economic-political context. But that isn't necessarily the case.

Pegged Currencies

Smaller countries who have a "thin market" (low demand) for their currency, may *peg* their currency to the value of another currency. For example, many economies in Latin America have pegged their currency exchange rate to the U.S. dollar. This is a somewhat arbitrary way to stabilize a currency, which would otherwise be swinging wildly in value, as well as creating problems for exporters and importers of the smaller countries. As most smaller economies don't have good reporting and transparency for the market to determine a value, they peg. However, pegging can become a problem for the smaller countries if their currency gets too far out of line with the realities of its economy.

The Special Case of China

As most everyone knows, the Chinese economy has been a wonderful story as the world's most populous country turned more to certain capitalistic policies and has been growing at an annual growth rate three to four times more rapid than the developed nations. This has been accomplished through a super aggressive policy of exports and state support. Low prices and acceptable quality has made China an economic powerhouse. The Chinese have been so successful that they are loaded with foreign credits from their trading partners. Eventually they need to exchange all their export revenues to China's domestic currency – the renminbi (RMB). Because of the rapid growth of its economy, China would normally expect some strong domestic inflationary pressures as the Chinese central bank would have to print more domestic money to convert to the rapidly growing supply of foreign currencies. But by pegging the yuan (international Chinese currency) to the U.S. dollar, the world was forced to accept an exchange rate that matched a much more stable and lower growth economy. By being able to keep their currency exchange rate from increasing in value, the Chinese could maintain more competitive pricing. An artificially devalued currency and subsidized loans and shipping have done much to further the tremendous strides the Chinese economy has made. In 2007, the Chinese dual currency (RMB and Yuan) were unpegged and the Chinese currency increased over 10% over the U.S. dollar by August of 2007.

In summary, comparative advantage states that a country will focus production and trade on those products and services providing the most profitability. However, price and quality still play a powerful role in determining the real success of comparative advantage. That's why exchange rates and their effect on pricing is a very important factor; moreover, a nation's foreign exchange rate can be greatly influenced by domestic issues. As the world's economies become more and more globalized, each country's internal politics and fiscal-monetary policies will become even more important in international trade.

FOREX features the most heavily traded currencies in "currency pairs." By a matter of interrelationships, one can figure the exchange of other currencies even if they are not presented in pairs.

Table of major FOREX currency pairs

EUR/USD	↑1.36210	↑1.36230	200.4
USD/JPY	↑115.910	↑115.920	170.4
GBP/USD	↑2.01930	↑2.01980	82.2
USD/CHF	↑1.20840	↑1.20890	99
USD/CAD	↑1.05310	↑1.05350	79.1
NZD/USD	↑0.70140	↑0.70220	36.7
GBP/JPY	↑234.080	↑234.150	48.2
GBP/CHF	↑2.44070	↑2.44180	31.6
EUR/CHF	↑1.64620	↑1.64655	113.2
EUR/GBP	↑0.67420	↑0.67460	105.1
EUR/JPY	↑157.890	↑157.895	92.2
CAD/JPY	↑110.010	↑110.080	47.5
CHF/JPY	↑95.8600	↑95.9400	81.8
AUD/USD	↑0.82050	↑0.82090	71.4
AUD/JPY	↑95.1100	↑95.1700	74.1

EUR = Euro; USD = US dollar; JPY = Japanese yen; CHF = Swiss franc; GBP = British pound; CAD = Canadian dollar; AUD = Australian dollar

Note: Each country has its currency quoted on the FOREX

8.3 FOREIGN INVESTMENT

Capital in the form of money can come from many sources. One of the most important forms – particularly for developing nations – is from foreign sources. Most governments have found that it is much more efficient and feasible to promote outside funding to help development than to apply for assistance from aid development agencies. Development of infrastructure helps to promote supporting businesses that provide employment and much needed tax revenues for the home country. In years before, many developing countries were rife with corruption and xenophobia, which scared away foreign investment, but today there is a global realization that foreign investment and new technology are playing a key role in development and strengthening new markets.

After World War II, the USA was about the only significant economy left standing. But very quickly, the world realized that if there was to be a speedy recovery after the massive destruction of most of the world's economies, redevelopment of markets needed to take place as fast as possible. Like the Phoenix resurrected from ashes, Germany and Japan were "bootstrapped" with U.S.A. underwriting and administrative know-how to become two economic powerhouses within the same lifetime of those who were at one time locked in a fight to the death. That amazing feat demonstrated what well implemented foreign investment was capable of achieving. However, most likely due to cultural values and corruption, other attempts at "development loans" to other struggling countries have failed miserably. During the oil crisis of the 1970s and 80s, developing countries defaulted on trillions of dollars of development loans and those defaults still cast a dark shadow over most of Latin America and Africa. As the pendulum has swung away from government involvement in development, the only source of funding new larger projects could come through attracting private investment. As a result, enlightened countries began programs aimed at making their countries attractive to private investment. They changed ownership restrictions and promoted the idea that private investment was not seen as an intrusion into domestic life but as a way for the citizens and the society to grow. Supporting this new philosophy was the enticement of low labor costs and other tax incentives. Many foreign companies saw advantages in the acquisition of foreign companies or establishing foreign operations with the intent of lowering costs and developing new markets for already successful brands. These companies are now called transnational companies and include most of the major companies in the world. Not only does international expansion give the Transnationals new growth and profits but also exposure to local tax codes and incentives that may be favorable to the overall corporate bottom-line.

Another huge source for new foreign capital is the mutual fund sector. Investment funds began to place portions of their huge portfolios into higher risk-return overseas investments. These marginal investments really began bearing fruit in the 1990s as vast portions of the world's demographic started to emerge from poverty and underdevelopment. Since 1996, the emerging markets index has provided superior performance over stock market indexes of developed nations. Countries like China, India, Brazil, Russia, Indonesia, and Mexico have seen strong and continued growth for close to a decade and the monies behind private investment have been pouring in to fuel the rather spectacular growth and improving possibilities for huge new markets.

Needless to say, there are some concerns over the aspect of large, autonomous transnational companies and their local subsidiaries dictating local politics, cultural preferences and social structure. However, most impoverished citizens seem to prefer to have an income and possibilities for a better life for their children – at least for now. Perhaps it will be a transaction with the devil but there is also hope that through commercial ties, and improving opportunities for all, the world will become a safer and more prosperous place for citizens of all nations.

8.4 BALANCE OF PAYMENTS

To be able to track how well an economy is doing, international trade also must be tracked. The balance of payments (BOP) is an accounting of a country's international transactions over a certain time period, typically a calendar quarter or year. The balance of payments shows the sum of the transactions between individuals, businesses, and government agencies in a particular country and those with the rest of the world. Any transaction that causes money to flow into a country is a credit to its BOP account, and any transaction that causes money to flow out is a debit.

The BOP includes the current account, which mainly measures the flow of goods and services; the capital account, which consists of capital transfers and the acquisition and disposal of non-produced, non-financial assets; and the financial account, which records investment flow.

The Current Account

The current account is composed of four sub-accounts:

- Merchandise trade consists of all raw materials and manufactured goods bought, sold, or given away. Until mid-1993, this was the figure that was used when the "balance of trade" was reported in the media. As certain countries are major producers of services such as consulting, software (i.e., Microsoft) and investment banking services, the definition of merchandise had to be refined. Since then, the merchandise trade account has been combined with a second sub-account – services – to determine the total for the balance of trade.

- Services include tourism, transportation, engineering, and business services, such as law, management consulting, and accounting. Fees from patents and copyrights on new technology, software, books, and movies also are recorded in the service category.

- Income receipts include income derived from ownership of assets, such as dividends on holdings of stock and interest on securities by individuals, investment companies and mutual funds.

- Unilateral transfers represent one-way transfers of assets, such as worker remittances from abroad and direct foreign aid.

The Capital Account or capital transfers, include debt forgiveness and migrants' transfers (goods and financial assets accompanying migrants as they leave or enter the country). In addition, capital transfers include the transfer of title to fixed assets and the transfer of funds linked to the sale or acquisition of fixed assets, gift and inheritance taxes, death duties, uninsured damage to fixed assets, and legacies.

Acquisition and disposal of non-produced, non-financial assets represent the sales and purchases of non-produced assets, such as the rights to natural resources, and the sales and purchases of intangible assets, such as patents, copyrights, trademarks, franchises, and leases.

The Financial Account

The financial account records trade in assets such as business firms, bonds, stocks, and real estate. It has two categories:

- U.S.-owned assets abroad are divided into official reserve assets: government assets, and private assets. These assets include gold, foreign currencies, foreign securities, reserve position in the International Monetary Fund, U.S. credits and other long-term assets, direct foreign investment, and U.S. claims reported by U.S. banks.
- Foreign-owned assets in the United States are divided into foreign official assets and other foreign assets in the United States. These assets include U.S. government, agency, and corporate securities, direct investment, U.S. currency, and U.S. liabilities reported by U.S. banks.

8.5 BALANCE OF PAYMENTS DEFICIT AND SURPLUS

In theory, the current account should balance with the capital plus the financial accounts. The sum of the balance of payments statements should be zero. For example, when the United States buys more goods and services than it sells (a current account deficit), it must finance the difference by borrowing, or by selling more capital assets than it buys (a capital account surplus). A country with a persistent current account deficit is, therefore, effectively exchanging capital assets for goods and services. Large trade deficits mean that the country is borrowing from abroad. In the balance of payments, this appears as an inflow of foreign capital. In reality, the accounts do not exactly offset each other, because of statistical discrepancies, accounting conventions, and exchange rate movements that change the recorded value of transactions.

Some feel that a balance of payments deficit is a bad thing. But for some countries such as the USA, it shows that citizens of the country with a deficit have a wide variety of goods and services to choose from – including foreign sources. It also means that other countries are holding the currency of the deficit country and that usually means that holders may very well repatriate their currency by exchanging for goods and services from the deficit country. Again, the balance of payments is a picture of what has happened over a specific period of time and may not represent the true picture over a longer time interval. For example, the U.S. has a large trade deficit with China, but China may use its excess dollars to purchase U.S. treasury securities, U.S. goods and services and shares in U.S. corporations.

8.6 THE INTERNATIONAL FINANCIAL SYSTEM

Earlier in the book, we discussed the components of the modern financial system. The global financial system piggybacks on those components to act as a catalyst to promote international development and trade for all nations. The main players are the International Monetary Fund (IMF), the World trade Organization (WTO), the Bank for International Settlements (BIS) and individual country national agencies such as central banks and finance ministries.

The G-8 is an informal group made up of Canada, France, Germany, Italy, Russia, the United Kingdom and the United States. This informal organization of industrial countries has no formal standing and no function other than communication. As a result, the G-8 is not considered as part of the International Financial System.

8.7 MONETARY POLICY AND GLOBALIZATION

The growing internationalization of finance—often referred to as globalization—has its pros and cons. The potential benefits of international finance are fairly clear. First, access to worldwide capital markets that can help many countries meet financial needs, borrowing in bad times and lending in good times. Second, international markets can promote domestic investment and growth by allowing other countries to make investments in foreign markets to boost home-country company profits. This in turn promotes domestic growth for the host country. Third, globalization may enhance macroeconomic discipline—capital flows may police bad government behavior. For example, if a country doesn't control its inflation, foreign exchange and stock markets will chastise a country's ability to raise money (bonds) and dissuade foreign direct investment. Fourth, internationalization may discipline domestic regulators. The possibility of financial institutions changing the locale of their operations, or investors investing in foreign markets abroad, may constrain excessive domestic regulation. Fifth, internationalization will increase competition, and will lead to more efficient banking systems and cheaper securities offerings.

There are also some potential costs of globalization. First, markets are not politically correct, so a hostile or poorly performing country may fail to attract capital, and may experience capital outflows and unemployment. Second, the volatility of capital flows can quickly destabilize an economy, as was the case in the 1997 Korean crisis, where short-term international bank lending quickly dried up. Third, the entry of foreign institutions, while increasing competition and efficiency, can lead to the demise or absorption of local financial institutions. Fourth, the integration of the world's financial system can result in quick transmissions of economic shocks.

8.7 CONCLUSION

It is clear that harmonization and increasing external authority have greatly increased since the end of World War II and the demise of the Bretton Woods Agreement. The central role of the IMF, and the ancillary role of the World Bank, in monitoring and enforcing banking standards in the developing world has provided a positive backdrop for growth and development. No doubt, there is an inexorable pressure to harmonize the rules of international finance, and to increasingly delegate power to international organizations to formulate policies and procedures. Some fear the loss of the domestic ability to guide local economic destiny; however, the potential efficiency savings for international trade and development are substantial.

Appendix A

Basics of International Trade – Key Terms

Tariffs	Taxes on imports Increases cost of imported goods
Quotas	Limit on amount of specific import item
Subsidy	Government supports for an industry
Dumping	Sale of goods below market value
Trade Embargo	Ban on trade for political purpose
Trade Agreement	Establishes rules of trade; generally favorable
MFN Status	Nation receives all trade advantages other nations receive
Free Trade	Goods flow without government interference
Balance of Trade	Difference between value of imports and exports. Trade deficit/surplus
Exchange Rate	Value of one currency in terms of another

Basics of International Trade – Key Organizations

Created post-WWII to oversee economic/trade issues and coordinate national policies.

International Monetary Fund (IMF)

- Oversees global financial system
- Mission: "an organization of 185 countries, Montenegro being the 185th as of January 18th, 2007, working to foster global monetary cooperation, secure financial stability, facilitate international trade, promote high employment and sustainable economic growth, and reduce poverty."
- Basics
  - Provides short term loans to members
  - Manages economies of member states, if necessary
  - Stabilizes exchange rates
  - 185 members today (newest member = Montenegro)

World Bank

- Conglomerate of 5 international finance organizations
- Controlled by developing nations (President is always American)
- Focus on developing nations
- Makes long term loans for economic development and poverty reduction
- Frequently criticized by public

World Trade Organization (WTO)

- Establishes rules for international trade
- Resolves disputes between member nations – trade court
- Can impose tariffs or sanctions on members

Group of Eight (G8)

- Major industrialized nations that discuss economic issues, trade, and exchange rates
- Members: Canada, France, Germany, Italy, Japan, UK, US, and Russia
- No formal rule-making
- Represent 65% of world economy

Sample Test Questions

Chapter 1

1) Which of the following describes barter?

   A) The gifting of an item
   B) When someone agrees to do work for food
   C) When money is exchanged for an item
   D) When a receipt is exchanged for an item

The correct answer is B:) When someone agrees to do work for food.

2) When was the first recorded production of minting of currency?

   A) 1789 B.C.
   B) 10th century A.D.
   C) 640-630 B.C.
   D) Golden age of Greece

The correct answer is C:) 640-630 B.C.

3) What are the basic properties of money?

   A) Generally recognized and backed by gold
   B) Recognized markings and proper weight
   C) Portable and has a measure of value
   D) Issued by the government and a measure of value

The correct answer is C:) Portable and has a measure of value.

4) When and where was paper money first used?

   A) Great Britain, 1684 A.D.
   B) Mesopotamia 1780 B.C.
   C) USA, 1702
   D) China, 10th Century A.D.

The correct answer is D:) China, 10th Century A.D.

5) Who were the fist bankers who used gold as security?

   A) European goldsmiths
   B) Etruscan traders
   C) British pawnbrokers
   D) Nicaraguan shrimp fishermen

The correct answer is A:) European goldsmiths.

6) What is convertibility?

   A) The exchange of cattle for sheep
   B) Changing paper currency for metal change
   C) Exchanging a used bill for a new one
   D) Exchanging money for a commodity of equivalent value

The correct answer is D:) Exchanging money for a commodity of equivalent value.

7) When did the U.S. adopt the gold standard?

   A) 1776
   B) 1812
   C) 1900
   D) 1929

The correct answer is C:)1900.

8) When did the U.S. go off the gold standard?

   A) 1929
   B) 1995
   C) 1973
   D) 2000

The correct answer is C:) 1973.

9) Why did countries turn to the gold or silver standard?

   A) To prevent counterfeiting
   B) To control the printing of paper money
   C) To keep a stable value on paper money
   D) All of the above

The correct answer is D:) All of the above.

10) What does it mean that money is "fungible"?

    A) Susceptible to the growth of fungus
    B) Backed by gold or silver
    C) Can morph into new forms of money
    D) Used only locally

The correct answer is C:) Can morph into new forms of money.

Chapter 2

11) When and where were the first recorded banking laws?

    A) 1st Century Rome
    B) 1864 England
    C) 1760 B.C. Mesopotamia
    D) 1934 Breton Woods

The correct answer is C:) 1760 B.C. Mesopotamia.

12) What institutions first served as banks?

    A) Military garrisons
    B) Local magistrates
    C) Slave exchanges
    D) Temples and palaces

The correct answer is D:) Temples and palaces.

13) Who developed the "fractional reserve" concept?

    A) Goldsmiths and jewelers
    B) Lawyers
    C) Politicians
    D) Free Masons

The correct answer is A:) Goldsmiths and jewelers.

14) Why were central banks created?

   A) To locate banks in a central area
   B) Help control money supply and interest rates
   C) To control inflation
   D) To take the banking sector away from private control

The correct answer is B:) Help control money supply and interest rates.

15) When and where was the first central bank established?

   A) France; 1864
   B) Germany; 1325
   C) Mesopotamia; 1760 B.C.
   D) England; 1864

The correct answer is D:) England; 1864.

16) When was a central bank established in the U.S.?

   A) 1776
   B) 1812
   C) 1900
   D) 1913

The correct answer is D:) 1913.

17) Explain the fractional reserve system.

   A) The depositor keeps only a fraction of the deposit.
   B) The bank keeps a fraction of a deposit on premises or with the Fed.
   C) The bank keeps a fraction of a deposit and borrows funds from other banks or the Fed to multiply the amount of money it has to loan.
   D) The depositor can borrow funds on a fraction of the deposit left with the bank as collateral.

The correct answer is C:) The bank keeps a fraction of a deposit and borrows funds from other banks or the Fed to multiply the amount of money it has to loan.

18) How does a bank create a "phantom assets"?

A) By printing currency
B) By borrowing money from the Fed
C) By borrowing money from other banks
D) Borrowing money from the Fed and depositing a fraction of its deposits with the Fed bank

The correct answer is D:) Borrowing money from the Fed and depositing a fraction of its deposits with the Fed bank.

19) How do banks act as distribution points for the money supply?

A) Banks hand out currency
B) The Fed allows a bank to lend out more money than it has on deposit
C) Banks can borrow from other banks or the fed
D) The Fed prints more money

The correct answer is B:) The Fed allows a bank to lend out more money than it has on deposit.

20) What is a reserve requirement?

A) The amount of money a bank must have on hand or on deposit with the Fed
B) The amount of money a depositor must maintain
C) Bank surpluses on deposits
D) The amount of money a bank must have on hand as mandated by the Treasury Department

The correct answer is A:) The amount of money a bank must have on hand or on deposit with the Fed.

21) Why does the banking system work?

A) Careful administration by the Fed
B) Gold backing of the currency
C) Legal recourse
D) Trust between depositors and the bank that if needed, the bank will have sufficient assets on hand

The correct answer is D:) Trust between depositors and the bank that if needed, the bank will have sufficient assets on hand.

22) How much of the U.S. GDP is made up of consumerism (retail purchases)?

   A) 50%
   B) 90%
   C) 80%
   D) 40%

The correct answer is C:) 80%.

Chapter 3

23) Which is not a component of the world contemporary financial system?

   A) The Fed
   B) IMF
   C) United Nations
   D) BIS

The correct answer is C:) United Nations.

24) What is the main duty of the IMF?

   A) Provide emergency funds to central banks
   B) Help underdeveloped countries
   C) Help maintain stable exchange rates
   D) Enforce international banking laws

The correct answer is C:) Help maintain stable exchange rates.

25) Who owns the IMF?

   A) The U.S. and England
   B) The United Federation
   C) Central banks
   D) Member countries

The correct answer is D:) Member countries.

26) What is the BIS and what does it do?

    A) The Bank Interconnect Service; helps banks clear checks
    B) The Bureau of International Settlements; enforces loan agreements
    C) The Bank of International Settlements; makes loans to central banks and uses the SDR
    D) The Bureau of International Slander; helps hostile nations create bellicose statements

The correct answer is C:) The Bank of International Settlements; makes loans to central banks and uses the SDR.

27) What does the World Bank do?

    A) Dedicated to the service of the Industrial countries
    B) Helps provide funds to all of the world's countries
    C) Provides technical and development funds for projects of member countries
    D) Provides financial and technical assistance to developing countries

The correct answer is D:) Provides financial and technical assistance to developing countries.

28) Which of the following is not a duty of a Central Bank?

    A) Collect taxes from other banks
    B) Conduct monetary policy
    C) Pursue full employment and stable prices
    D) Supervise banking institutions

The correct answer is A:) Collect taxes from other banks.

29) Who owns the U.S. Federal Reserve Banking System?

    A) The U.S. Government
    B) Private shareholders of member banks
    C) The Department of the Treasury
    D) A consortium of international banks

The correct answer is B:) Private shareholders of member banks.

30) What is the main difference between an investment bank and a commercial bank?

   A) An investment bank makes loans to the general public
   B) A commercial bank provides services only to businesses
   C) An investment bank works closely with the SEC (Securities and Exchange Commission)
   D) Commercial banks are state chartered

The correct answer is C:) An investment bank works closely with the SEC (Securities and Exchange Commission).

31) What is the main difference between the FOREX and a commodity exchange?

   A) The FOREX is dedicated to trading currencies only
   B) The Commodity exchanges are limited to commodities only
   C) The FOREX is limited to large institutions
   D) Commodities do not include currencies

The correct answer is A:) The FOREX is dedicated to trading currencies only.

32) What is equity financing?

   A) When a company sells equipment to obtain cash
   B) A bank lends funds to a business
   C) A company sells shares to investors but retains ownership
   D) A company sells shares of ownership to investors

The correct answer is D:) A company sells shares of ownership to investors.

33) What is one of the main concerns about today's financial system?

   A) The U.S. controls the system
   B) Developing countries will absorb the lending capacity
   C) The system is too removed from reality
   D) The complexity and growing interconnectedness between elements of the system may make the whole system vulnerable to a "domino effect" if just one or two of the components fail

The correct answer is D:) The complexity and growing interconnectedness between elements of the system may make the whole system vulnerable to a "domino effect" if just one or two of the components fail.

34) What does securitization mean?

   A) Entering into a contract for security services
   B) Loans—usually mortgages—are packaged up and sold to investors
   C) Turning a usually illiquid asset into cash by selling the future income of the assets for cash
   D) Putting a convicted banker in jail

The correct answer is C:) Turning a usually illiquid asset into cash by selling the future income of the assets for cash.

35) What is Freddie Mack?

   A) A hamburger named for a famous California skateboarder
   B) The name of a Federal Bank
   C) A GSE
   D) A federal loan program

The correct answer is C:) A GSE.

36) Why would an importer purchase a currency future contract?

   A) To protect the purchasing power of local currency
   B) To take advantage of lower exchange rates
   C) To demonstrate commitment to the overseas exporter
   D) Used as security for a bank loan

The correct answer is A:) To protect the purchasing power of local currency.

37) What is a Mutual Fund?

   A) A fund dedicated to the buying mutuals
   B) An investment fund made up of pooled funds
   C) An investment vehicle that allows investors to buy portions of shares of stock of a variety of companies
   D) Limited to wealthy investors, it is managed by a board of directors

The correct answer is C:) An investment vehicle that allows investors to buy portions of shares of stock of a variety of companies.

38) What is a Hedge Fund?

   A) A fund that attempts to make investments which will make profits when the market is in a counter move
   B) An investment vehicle that specializes in risky investments
   C) A fund devoted to keeping a company's landscape in good condition
   D) A mutual fund for only wealthy investors

The correct answer is A:) A fund that attempts to make investments which will make profits when the market is in a counter move.

Chapter 4

39) What best describes the effect of interest rates?

   A) The money needed to finance a project
   B) The amount charged by a bank for borrowing money
   C) The cost of money
   D) A measurement of prices

The correct answer is C:) The cost of money.

40) What is the best definition of "inflation"?

   A) The cost of borrowing money
   B) Increase in wholesale prices
   C) Erosion of the value of money
   D) Decreasing PPI

The correct answer is C:) Erosion of the value of money.

41) What does an increasing PPI mean?

   A) Lower prices in the future
   B) Higher prices at the retail level
   C) An increase in GDP
   D) Increasing wholesale prices

The correct answer is D:) Increasing wholesale prices.

42) Which has more inflationary impact?

   A) Increasing GDP
   B) Higher interest rates
   C) Higher CPI
   D) Lower PPI

The correct answer is C:) Higher CPI.

43) What does not help to hold down inflation?

   A) Higher interest rates
   B) Lower PPI
   C) Lower interest rates
   D) Lower CPI

The correct answer is C:) Lower interest rates.

44) Increasing globalization will most probably do which of the following:

   A) Drive up prices
   B) Reduce pressure on the PPI
   C) Increase pressure on the PPI
   D) Help keep CPI down through increased competition

The correct answer is D:) Help keep CPI down through increased competition.

45) Ideally, how will globalization help industrialized nations?

   A) Increase the markets for goods and services as buying power of developing markets creates new demand
   B) Displace workers in industrialized nations
   C) Increase Government revenues by the increasing tariff revenues
   D) Devalue the local currency

The correct answer is A:) Increase the markets for goods and services as buying power of developing markets creates new demand.

46) What is the meaning of "present value"?

   A) The value of today's dollar
   B) How much would be needed to be invested in today's money to have a specific value in the future given a certain interest rate
   C) The future value of today's money invested at a certain interest rate
   D) How much needs to be invested to have an equivalent amount in the future

The correct answer is B:) How much would be needed to be invested in today's money to have a specific value in the future given a certain interest rate.

47) When would you want to know "future value"?

   A) When you want to know how much money you would make on in investment
   B) How much an investment would cost you today to yield a certain amount in the future
   C) The effects of inflation on the future value of money
   D) Return on an investment over a certain period of time at a certain interest rate

The correct answer is D:) Return on an investment over a certain period of time at a certain interest rate.

48) What is an example of "opportunity cost"?

   A) What an investment will cost in terms of interest charges
   B) What it cost to not invest
   C) A payment made under the table to get access to an opportunity
   D) The difference between two different investments

The correct answer is B:) What it cost to not invest.

49) You invest in a money market account which pays you 2.5% in interest. You could have invested in a mutual fund which would have given a return of over 12% over the same time period. The difference between the two investments is 9.5%. What is this differential called?

   A) Missed gain
   B) Investment choice alternative cost (ICAC)
   C) Bad choice
   D) Opportunity cost of not owning the mutual fund

The correct answer is D:) Opportunity cost of not owning the mutual fund.

50) High interest rates could be an indication of…

   A) Low inflation
   B) Low demand
   C) High inflation
   D) High loan demand

The correct answer is C:) High inflation.

51) What is the Fed Discount rate?

   A) The rate a bank charges the Federal Reserve Bank to borrow money
   B) The rate that the Fed Reserve Bank charges a member bank to make a direct loan from the Fed
   C) The rate banks can lend to other banks
   D) The rate that a bank can lend money to good customers

The correct answer is B:) The rate that the Fed Reserve Bank charges a member bank to make a direct loan from the Fed.

52) What is the Prime rate?

   A) The rate a bank charges the Federal Reserve Bank to borrow money
   B) The rate that the Fed Reserve Bank charges its best customers
   C) The rate banks can lend to other banks
   D) The rate that a bank will lend money to good customers

The correct answer is D:) The rate that a bank will lend money to good customers.

53) What is the Fed Funds rate?

   A) The rate a bank charges the Federal Reserve Bank to borrow money
   B) The rate that the Fed Reserve Bank charges a member bank to make a direct loan from the Fed
   C) The rate banks can lend to other banks
   D) The rate that a bank can lend money to good customers

The correct answer is C:) The rate banks can lend to other banks.

54) Why are interest rates on some government bonds important to banks?

    A) It means a bank must pay more to borrow money from the government
    B) Consumers will decrease spending
    C) It mirrors inflation
    D) Some consumer loans are tied to the changes is some government bond issues

The correct answer is D:) Some consumer loans are tied to the changes is some government bond issues.

55) What is a Reserve Requirement?

    A) Amount a bank needs to always have on deposit
    B) The amount a bank needs to have on deposit or paid to the Fed to borrow money from the Fed or other banks
    C) The amount the Fed must have on deposit
    D) The amount of money an account must have on balance

The correct answer is B:) The amount a bank needs to have on deposit or paid to the Fed to borrow money from the Fed or other banks.

56) Normally, the interest on credit cards is based on the interest rate of which instrument?

    A) Short-term government treasury bill
    B) Home mortgage rates
    C) Fed prime rate
    D) Discount rate

The correct answer is A:) Short-term government treasury bill.

57) Indirect financing is…

    A) Having a friend get a loan for you
    B) Getting a loan guaranteed by a parent
    C) Getting a loan from a bank
    D) Getting a loan from an uncle

The correct answer is C:) Getting a loan from a bank.

58) Direct financing is…

   A) When you ask for a loan from a bank
   B) When a company sells shares on a stock exchange
   C) When a company borrows money from the Fed
   D) When a government makes a loan to the Central Bank

The correct answer is B:) When a company sells shares on a stock exchange.

59) How does a bank make the majority of its income?

   A) Selling real estate
   B) Making loans to other banks
   C) Using depositor funds to make loans and charge interest on the loans
   D) By investing in socks and bonds

The correct answer is C:) Using depositor funds to make loans and charge interest on the loans.

60) Banks act as a distribution point for what?

   A) Credit cards
   B) Money
   C) Home mortgages
   D) Auto loans

The correct answer is B:) Money.

61) What service can a bank not offer to its customers?

   A) Sale of gold
   B) Stock and bond brokerage
   C) Insurance
   D) Motorcycle loan

The correct answer is A:) Sale of gold.

62) Normally, when we make a deposit, the bank will normally do what?

   A) Make a loan to a customer for the full deposit amount
   B) Package the deposit and sell the package to a GSE
   C) Use the deposit to leverage a loan from another bank or the Fed
   D) Make a digital credit and send the cash to the Fed

The correct answer is C:) Use the deposit to leverage a loan from another bank or the Fed.

63) Typically, a bank can leverage how much money from a deposit?

   A) 2x
   B) 3x
   C) 6x
   D) 10x

The correct answer is D:) 10x.

64) Which system represents the way banks create money?

   A) The Federal Reserve System
   B) The Breton Woods method
   C) The Frictional Reserve System
   D) The Fractional Reserve System

The correct answer is D:) The Fractional Reserve System.

65) What does it mean when a bank says it has deposit insurance?

   A) It means that you can apply for deposit insurance
   B) It means that you have $10,000 of coverage for life insurance
   C) It means that you are automatically covered for up to $10,000 if the bank goes bankrupt
   D) It means that you are automatically covered for up to $100,000 for each account if the bank goes bankrupt

The correct answer is D:) It means that you are automatically covered for up to $100,000 for each account if the bank goes bankrupt.

66) What is a "run" on a bank?

   A) A bank sponsored marathon
   B) When the Fed has cause to make a surprise inspection of a bank's records
   C) When bank customers converge at the same time to ask for a withdrawal of deposits
   D) When interest rates go up

The correct answer is C:) When bank customers converge at the same time to ask for a withdrawal of deposits.

67) Why do some investors require an offshore bank?

   A) Privacy
   B) Tax free investments
   C) Access to new capital markets
   D) No eligibility restrictions

The correct answer is A:) Privacy.

68) Which type of bank would you choose if wanting to open a money market account?

   A) An Investment bank
   B) A private bank
   C) An offshore bank
   D) A commercial bank

The correct answer is D:) A commercial bank.

69) An investment bank would most likely be involved with…

   A) An IRA
   B) An SSA
   C) An IPO
   D) A 401(k)

The correct answer is C:) An IPO.

70) What is meant by the term "equity financing"?

    A) Financing from an equity company
    B) When a public company sells equipment to raise operating cash
    C) Financing in equal parts
    D) Financing by selling ownership rights

The correct answer is D:) Financing by selling ownership rights.

71) Which form of company specializes in local development?

    A) An Investment bank
    B) An investment company or syndicate
    C) A leverage buyout company
    D) A mutual fund

The correct answer is B:) An investment company or syndicate.

72) What is a venture capitalist?

    A) A person who lends money to high risk ventures
    B) A person or company who lends money-normally to a private company-to enable it to go public
    C) An individual who lends money in exchange for stock
    D) A company or person who makes money only when a company goes public

The correct answer is B:) A person or company who lends money-normally to a private company-to enable it to go public.

73) A heavy machinery company may most likely choose which type of company to do financing of new machinery?

    A) An investment company
    B) An Investment bank
    C) A commercial bank
    D) A leasing company

The correct answer is D:) A leasing company.

74) When a person purchases a home but lacks enough for the total down payment, what might they be looking for?

   A) A first mortgage
   B) An equity loan
   C) A line of credit
   D) A second mortgage

The correct answer is D:) A second mortgage.

75) If a home buyer can't qualify for a loan from a bank, they might look for…

   A) Subprime lender
   B) Credit Union
   C) Investment bank
   D) Equity financing

The correct answer is A:) Subprime lender.

76) When a company sells its account receivables (monies owed the company) to a company in exchange for cash, this is known as…

   A) An asset backed loan
   B) A cash advance
   C) A leaseback arrangement
   D) A mortgage

The correct answer is A:) An asset backed loan.

77) When a company pledges a part of its inventory in exchange for cash, it is known as…

   A) Asset backed loan
   B) Inventory loan
   C) Capital advance
   D) Line of credit

The correct answer is A:) Asset backed loan.

78) Asset backed loans are…

    A) A loan of first choice
    B) Used as a last resort form of financing
    C) Usually has a lower interest rate than a bank loan
    D) In the case of pledging accounts receivable, is also known as "factoring"

The correct answer is D:) In the case of pledging accounts receivable, is also known as "factoring."

79) The main responsibility of the Fed is…

    A) Promote high employment
    B) Promote low inflation
    C) Control money supply
    D) Prevent and mediate any potential economic financial crisis

The correct answer is D:) Prevent and mediate any potential economic financial crisis.

80) The Fed was established because of…

    A) A financial crisis in 1907
    B) The Central Bank act of 1907
    C) Unanimous agreement of Congress in 1912
    D) Promoted by Ludwig Von Meises

The correct answer is A:) A financial crisis in 1907.

81) The Fed gained greatly in importance after the economic crisis caused by…

    A) World War II
    B) Oil crisis of the 1970's
    C) The Civil War
    D) The Suez canal crisis

The correct answer is B:) Oil crisis of the 1970's.

82) During the oil crisis, inflation in the U.S. reached as high as…

   A) 13.5%
   B) 18%
   C) 10%
   D) 23%

The correct answer is A:) 13.5%.

83) The Federal Reserve System is composed of…

   A) One central bank and 12 regional banks
   B) One central bank
   C) 12 regional banks
   D) 50 banks representing each state

The correct answer is C:) 12 regional banks.

84) The chairman of the Fed is…

   A) Elected by the board of governors
   B) Appointed by the Congress
   C) Appointed by the President of the U.S.
   D) Elected by member banks

The correct answer is C:) Appointed by the President of the U.S.

85) What component of the Fed oversees and influences overall monetary and credit?

   A) The FOMC
   B) The Board of Governors
   C) The Comptroller General
   D) The Central Bank

The correct answer is A:) The FOMC.

86) The Fed will raise interest rates by…

   A) Purchasing securities on the open market
   B) Selling bonds on the open market
   C) Ordering banks to raise their Prime rate
   D) Lowering the Reserve Requirement

The correct answer is B:) Selling bonds on the open market.

87) By raising and lowering interest rates, the Fed tries to influence...

   A) Bank demand for money
   B) Government spending
   C) Aggregate demand
   D) Savings rate

The correct answer is C:) Aggregate demand.

88) The Fed is constantly balancing the following elements:

   A) Interest rates and unemployment
   B) Money supply, interest rates and aggregate savings
   C) Money supply, interest rates, inflation and aggregate demand
   D) Balance of payments, inflation, savings rates and inflation

The correct answer is C:) Money supply, interest rates, inflation and aggregate demand.

89) Who is the "lender of last resort"?

   A) The Sultan of Brunei
   B) The World Bank
   C) The U.S. Government
   D) The Fed

The correct answer is D:) The Fed.

90) When a nation focuses on its most efficient production, it is practicing...

   A) Conspicuous consumption
   B) Trade optimization
   C) Comparative advantage
   D) Ricardo's Axiom

The correct answer is C:) Comparative advantage.

91) The concept of comparative advantage was developed by...

   A) Adam Smith
   B) Paul Samuels
   C) Anthony Soprano
   D) David Ricardo

The correct answer is D:) David Ricardo.

92) A pegged currency is when a country…

   A) Sets a specific exchange rate with every other country
   B) Ties its currency exchange rate to that of another country
   C) Allows its currency to be determined by the market
   D) Prints only a specific quantity of money

The correct answer is B:) Ties its currency exchange rate to that of another country.

93) What is a floating currency?

   A) When a nation's currency is allowed to adjust to the market
   B) When a currency is pegged to another nation's exchange rate
   C) The value of a nation's currency is decided by the market
   D) The Central bank decides what the exchange rate will be

The correct answer is C:) The value of a nation's currency is decided by the market.

94) When an importer purchases a certain amount of foreign currency for a delivery to be made in several months, it is called…

   A) A futures exchange
   B) A FOREX purchase
   C) A Tranche
   D) A futures contract

The correct answer is D:) A futures contract.

95) If the central bank of a nation increases interest rates, what may be the effect on the nation's exchange rate?

   A) The exchange rate will go up in relation to most currencies
   B) Will have no effect on exchange rates
   C) The exchange rate will go down in relation to most currencies
   D) The domestic value of the money will go up also

The correct answer is A:) The exchange rate will go up in relation to most currencies.

96) What is the reason for the answer in question #95?

    A) Less demand for the nation's currency
    B) More demand for the nation's currency because investors may want to invest in the country to benefit from higher comparative interest rates
    C) Decreased demand for the nation's goods
    D) More countries will sell the reserves of the currency

The correct answer is B:) More demand for the nation's currency because investors may want to invest in the country to benefit from higher comparative interest rates.

97) What is the advantage of having a devaluing currency?

    A) Imported goods will be less expensive
    B) There is no advantage
    C) Exported goods will be less expensive and thus more competitive
    D) Domestic prices will move lower

The correct answer is C:) Exported goods will be less expensive and thus more competitive.

98) What private investment vehicle has done most to provide growth for the developing world?

    A) Venture Capitalists
    B) Commercial Banks
    C) Charitable contributions
    D) Mutual Funds

The correct answer is D:) Mutual Funds.

99) The balance of payments is…

    A) The surplus or deficit that a country has with another
    B) The surplus or deficit of a nation with the rest of the world
    C) The flow of goods and services being exported by a nation
    D) Surplus or deficit of foreign currency reserves

The correct answer is B:) The surplus or deficit of a nation with the rest of the world.

100) What is a potential risk of globalization?

   A) One nation dominating the world
   B) A transfer of wealth from the developed world to the underdeveloped
   C) An unforeseen financial crisis which could affect the entire world
   D) The Sultan of Brunei could become the Sultan of the World

The correct answer is C:) An unforeseen financial crisis which could affect the entire world.

 # Test-Taking Strategies

Here are some test-taking strategies that are specific to this test and to other DSST tests in general:

- Keep your eyes on the time. Pay attention to how much time you have left.
- Read the entire question and read all the answers. Many questions are not as hard to answer as they may seem. Sometimes, a difficult sounding question really only is asking you how to read an accompanying chart. Chart and graph questions are on most DANTES/DSST tests and should be an easy free point.
- If you don't know the answer immediately, the new computer-based testing lets you mark questions and come back to them later if you have time.
- Read the wording carefully. Some words can give you hints to the right answer. There are no exceptions to an answer when there are words in the question such as always, all or none. If one of the answer choices includes most or some of the right answers, but not all, then that is not the answer. Here is an example:

    The primary colors include all of the following:
    A) Red, Yellow, Blue, Green
    B) Red, Green, Yellow
    C) Red, Orange, Yellow
    D) Red, Yellow, Blue

    Although item A includes all the right answers, it also includes an incorrect answer, making it incorrect. If you didn't read it carefully, were in a hurry, or didn't know the material well, you might fall for this.

- Make a guess on a question that you do not know the answer to. There is no penalty for an incorrect answer. Eliminate the answer choices that you know are incorrect. For example, this will let your guess be a 1 in 3 chance instead.

 # Test Preparation

How much you need to study depends on your knowledge of a subject area. If you are interested in literature, took it in school, or enjoy reading then your study and preparation for the literature or humanities test will not need to be as intensive as that of someone who is new to literature.

This book is much different than the regular DANTES study guides. This book actually teaches you the information that you need to know to pass the test. If you are particularly interested in an area, or feel that you want more information, do a quick search online. We've tried not to include too much depth in areas that are not as essential on the test. Everything in this book will be on the test. It is important to understand all major theories and concepts listed in the table of contents. It is also important to know any bolded words.

Don't worry if you do not understand or know a lot about the area. With minimal study, you can complete and pass the test.

One of the fallacies of other test books is test questions. People assume that the content of the questions are similar to what will be on the test. That is not the case. They are only there to test your "test taking skills" so for those who know to read a question carefully, there is not much added value from taking a "fake" test.

To prepare for the test, make a series of goals. Allot a certain amount of time to review the information you have already studied and to learn additional material. Take notes as you study; it will help you learn the material.

Legal Note

All rights reserved. This Study Guide, Book and Flashcards are protected under the US Copyright Law. No part of this book or study guide or flashcards may be reproduced, distributed or stored in a retrieval system, or transmitted in any form or by any means, electronic, mechanical, photocopying, recording, or otherwise, without the prior written permission of the publisher Breely, Crush & Associates LLC.

FLASHCARDS

This section contains flashcards for you to use to further your understanding of the material and test yourself on important concepts, names or dates. You can cut these out to study from or keep them in the study guide, flipping the page over to check yourself.

Tobacco leaves were used as what	LETS
Reserve requirement	GDP
IMF	OPEC
FOMC	SEC

Local Exchange Trading System	Fiat money
Gross Domestic Product	The current amount that a bank must have on hand to cover anticipated withdrawals
Organization of Oil Exporting Countries	International Monetary Fund
Securities and Exchange Commission	Federal Open Market Committee

Securitization	IPO
Mutual Funds	Inflation
CPI	Present value of money
Future value of money	Future value formula

Initial public offering	Packaging pools of loans or receivables for redistribution to investors
Erosion of the value of money over time	Pooled funds which are professionally managed to optimize returns on a flexible investment portfolio
The amount of money you have now in comparison to how much you will need for a future expenditure	Consumer Price Index
$FV = P * (1+i)^n$	The future amount of money you will have based on current interest rates over a set period of time

Spread	Fed funds rates
Direct financing	Indirect financing
A run on a bank is when	Offshore banking
Leveraged buyouts	CDs

Determine the rate at which banks lend money to each other	The difference between the Fed Funds rate and retail loan rates
Borrowing from a bank who acts as an agent for the depositors of the bank	Borrowing from one source or individual
Usually operates with the main intent of providing banking secrecy and less regulatory restrictions	Depositors panic
Certificates of deposit	LBOs

Charter	NOW
IRA	Escrow account
Sub-prime lender lends higher or lower than prime?	Thin market
Yuan	Balance of payments

Negotiable order of withdrawal	A formal document that governs the manner in which the bank is regulated and operated
Giving money to a neutral third party, generally involved in real estate transactions	Individual retirement accounts
Low demand	Higher rates than prime
BOP	International Chinese currency

World Trade Organization	**BIS**
G-8	**Tariffs**
Quotas	**Subsidy**
Dumping	**Trade Embargo**

Bank for International Settlements	WTO
Taxes on imports	Informal group made up of Canada, France, Germany, Italy, Russia, UK and US
Government supports for an industry	Limit on amount of specific import item
Ban on trade for political purpose	Sale of goods below market value

Trade Agreement	MFN Status
Free Trade	Balance of Trade
Exchange Rate	Which European country does not use the Euro?
When inventory is high, prices are more likely to rise or drop?	Loan collateral

Nation receives all trade advantages others nations receive	Establish rules of trade; generally favorable
Difference between value of imports and exports; trade deficit/surplus	Goods flow without government interference
UK	Value of one currency in terms of another
Something of value (property, etc.) to secure a loan	Drop